Ten Keys to Living a Soul Life

Suzie Bowers, CHT

Soul Discovery Coach

http://www.suziebowers.com

By reading this document, you assume all risks associated with using the advice given below, with a full understanding that you, solely, are responsible for your own experience. Author does not dispense or give medical advice. The intent of the author is to offer information of a general nature that may help you in your quest for spiritual and emotional well-being. Anything that may occur as a result of putting this information into action in any way, and regardless of the interpretation of the advice is the sole responsibility of the reader. The author and the publisher assume no responsibility for your actions.

Suzie Bowers Publishing

1625 W. March Lane, Suite 101

Stockton, California 95209

Suziebowers@yahoo.com ~ 800-758-1239

ISBN-13: 978-1456350321

ISBN-10: 1456350323

Dedication

I would like to dedicate this book to my children, Kyle, Kody and Braeden. Thanks for bringing so much joy into my life. You have taught me every day about laughter, unconditional love and have given me many opportunities to grow and evolve as a person, as a soul. Thank you.

Fly and be free, embrace all this world has to offer. You can accomplish anything you choose.

I love you.

Acknowledgments

Not much can be learned and experienced without the helping hand of many other souls.

I would like to say thank you, first to my husband Stuart, whose friendship and support has made possible all the things I've dared to try over the years in my search for understanding why we're here and why we feel the way we do. And, I must say, there's been a lot.

Thank you to my best friend and sister, Heidi Moorefield whose loving and gentle spirit has been a tremendous blessing…I am so grateful.

I'd also like to thank my mother and father, who always encouraged me to try new things, to keep an open mind and be happy no matter what. And even in their dysfunction, taught me so much about life.

I must acknowledge all the teachers whom I have studied and listened to, all the pioneers that have courageously forged the trails ahead of all of us.

Anthony Robbins, Dr. Wayne Dyer, Ph.D., Lynn V. Andrews, Doreen Virtue, Ph.D., Gregg Braden, Dr. Deepak Chopra, Eckart Tolle, Oprah Winfrey, Napoleon Hill, Dr. Joseph Murphy, Jose Silva, Louise Hay, Sanaya

Roman and Duane Packer, Jennifer Grainger, Don Miguel Ruiz, Debbie Ford, Carlos Castaneda, Lynn McTaggart, Starhawk, Jesus, Buddha, Desiree' Heinen, Dr. Masaru Emoto, Rhonda Byrne and all the cast of The Secret, Sonia Choquette, Silver Ravenwolf, Amber Wolfe, Barbara Brennan, and all the Angels, Guides, Masters and Beings of Light who are always watching over and guiding me.

There are so many more, the list is too long to continue.

I'd also like to say a very special thank you to the life work of James DiGirolomo whose passing this year was a serious shock. Finding Jim and his school of Wisdom Center Technologies was a major turning point in my life. Six months of hands on training in metaphysics and hypnotherapy with Jim was instrumental in uplifting my life, facilitating my own healing process and the hundreds of others I've been blessed to work with. Jim was "the light," and all who knew him experienced the beauty of his enlightened spirit. I must say, other than Dr. Wayne Dyer, Jim was the closest I have ever been to a fully actualized human being.

Contents

Introduction
"Namaste'"

Namaste' is an ancient Sanskrit blessing which means:

"I honor the place in you where Spirit dwells. I honor the place in you, which is of love, of light, of truth, of peace. When you are in that place in you and I am in that place in me, we are ONE."

For me, the word "Namaste'" is the essence of soul consciousness, the recognition of the divine spark within each of us. When we maintain a level of higher consciousness, a connection to the Divine Source of who we are and all that is, we truly begin to live our lives in the most joyful, healthy, successful way. From the Soul's perspective we are all one – originating from the same source of All That Is.

One thing I know about you, is that you are a pioneer into a way of thinking and being that many will scoff at. For some it's easier to just stay stuck in misery and take another Prozac.TM

I am willing to bet that you are not like that, or if you have needed to go that route, like many others have had to, perhaps now you are ready to explore a different approach.

You and I are kindred spirits, seekers of inner knowledge and wisdom, which is why you have been drawn to this book. I am grateful to you for embarking on this journey of self-discovery, to explore the concept that there may be something better available to us than what we've been taught to accept as reality! Congratulations for your willingness to try something different.

Thank you for taking your time to check out this book. I am excited and delighted to share with you, what I have learned and experienced personally as a mother, a friend, a hypnotherapist, soul discovery coach and really, from just life in general. After working with approximately a hundred different people, from all areas or walks of life, I discovered a common theme: everyone wants to be happy, or at least says they do, and we seem to be wired in a way that makes finding true happiness a challenging proposition. The good news is: we can rewire ourselves and utilize our innate strengths.

I too, have at times, found true happiness to be difficult to hang on to when I'm constantly reacting to my outside circumstances instead of going within to find the peace and joy that is inherently a large part of my natural being.

And it was through a process of an injured body and deep depression, following a horse-back riding accident, which I too, looked for resources besides the standard prescription drug answer. I was very fortunate to be led to a hypnotherapist and my journey of self-healing and self-empowerment began.

What I learned is that looking out into the world of chaos and negativity for joy is like trying to make cookies without the sugar.

I have also discovered that what we focus on is what we get more of. So focusing on sadness and negativity and what isn't working, only gives us more of that.

True joy should be and is something as natural as breathing. We then must ask the question: Is it our environment that creates our dissatisfaction? Is it the circumstances that we find ourselves in? Is it our upbringing? Is it the world's tendency to focus on chaos and negativity? Is it that in creating conveniences, which were supposed to give us more time for ourselves, we actually have manifested less time to do what we enjoy? Are we inherently drawn to dramatize situations in order to feel good about ourselves? Is it our need to be right about what we believe or is it the need to make someone else wrong that drives us? Why do we complicate things?

This is just a small sample of the questions that we can ask and will explore in this book. Hopefully, this will give us something to think about that will open our minds to other possibilities.

There have been numerous books and programs regarding the topic of how to be happy, how to be successful in life. In search for the inner meaning of our experience and why we behave the way we do or feel the way we feel, humans have created untold techniques, therapies, drugs, and ways to heal ourselves that seem to justify our very existence. Yet, even with hundreds, perhaps thousands of books and coaching programs available to us, prosperity, happiness, love and even health elude so many. If "how tos" were enough, we'd all have what we desire.

Some believe it is our self-esteem that is at the root of our problems, others think it may be brain chemical imbalances.

In our search for answers we've developed, psychotherapy, talk therapy, inner child work, rebirthing, EFT, neuro-linguistic programming, cry therapy, scream therapy, regression therapy, hypnotherapy and anti-depressants…well you get the point.

Through all these modalities the common thread that seems to link all the other modalities is the importance of consciousness. It's through the awakened consciousness that we find the inherent tools we already have within us to create the life we desire and deserve. The awakened consciousness leads us to our Soul, the very essence of who we truly are. When we live as our Soul, we have a deeper awareness of the connection to the Divine Source of All That Is. It is in that awareness and connection that our energy vibration is elevated and we can access the infinite possibilities available to us and tap into our unlimited potential.

I call this – Living a Soul Life.

What does this mean? As I previously stated, it means moving through the world connected with the Divine Spirit, looking at every experience as an opportunity to grow and making the conscious choice to live joyfully and more fully in every possible moment.

Living a Soul Life means living *your* truth. Not your parent's truth or your teacher or your pastor's truth or the truth that's right for your husband, wife or your friends. It's about giving yourself permission to be happy, follow your own guidance and traveling the path that fuels the passion inside of you. In order to move toward what we desire, it is also critical to forgive ourselves for our so-called mistakes and completely, wholly, release the past.

Sounds simple, doesn't it?

Yet, being truly, conscious in every moment and consistently happy can be very elusive, especially for those who choose to stay "asleep," in a victim mentality and reacting to the world. Those who do not hold the keys in their hand like you do now and are probably not even looking for them, do not know that there is another way. Either way the road can be a bumpy one, but navigating the path with a conscious awareness gives you back your power. This power is already yours, and you have a choice: remain shrouded in the drama of life or choose to be happy and accept responsibility for co-creating your experience from a higher level of understanding.

Spirit manifests itself uniquely in each one of us.

Living from the Soul level is about learning to live your life from the wise, loving, perspective of your Soul and Higher Self, where everything is about joy, personal growth, health and evolution. It's about living your life on the purpose that is right for *you*, regardless of what others think, regardless of what's going on "out there," regardless of circumstances that may be going on in your life at any given moment. In essence, it's about living your passion and accepting responsibility for *every* experience.

From the wise and unconditionally loving perspective of your Soul, there's no such thing as failure – everything and every experience is an opportunity for human and spiritual growth and learning. Every experience and interaction is an opportunity to express unconditional love and forgiveness. But you cannot give what you do not have inside you already, so this journey to wholeness starts within you.

"I'm not just a human being. I am a spiritual being, having a human experience."

When we intend to look at things from this consciousness expanding perspective, we can truly tap into the wisdom of our Soul or Divine Self and also accept ourselves as we are and as the co-creators of our reality. This is where the journey to true happiness begins and can be grasped in an ongoing way. A delicious peace can permeate every molecule of your body.

Living a Soul Life is really about living in the essence, the spirit of joy. It means staying connected to a higher flow, to your immortal self and the ***Source*** of your immortal self. And it's being able to open up to the idea and recognize that you are an immortal spirit having a human experience. Living a Soul Life is about stepping into your immortal power.

How do we do this? That's what we're going to explore in this book and also in my self-improvement series – Monday Morning Power Start. http://www.suziebowers.com.

True success in life, whether you desire physical health, joy, financial success, or fantastic relationships, as I mentioned, begins on the path of "becoming conscious."

What does that really mean?

Becoming conscious is the doorway we must walk through in order to take us to the next level where we can choose to experience bliss more of the time.

For some of us this doorway will seem more like a birth canal as we squeeze ourselves through from one reality into another, from the darkness of fear and ignorance into the light of consciousness and acceptance.

Becoming conscious is a manner of living where we are the observer, allowing the outside circumstances to flow around us without getting reactive or involved on a personality level. In fact, it's about seeing everything and everyone beyond the illusion of the personality and from the higher, wiser perspective of the Soul or Divine Self, where everything is about growth and evolution.

I think we can all agree that one thing we know for sure, is that "stuff happens," personally and globally. What we focus on, however, is what we get more of. And now, with the internet, we have so many things available to distract us. As you read further and explore the 10 keys to living a soul life, to creating the life you desire and deserve, you will learn how to change your focus and direct it toward what you desire. As you focus on what you desire, instead of putting your energy into what you don't want, you will become very magnetic to the good you desire to manifest.

Understanding the power inherent within your own subconscious mind is the first and most important step you must take on your road to joy.

The awareness of how your thoughts create your experience will allow you to begin to shift old programs and limiting beliefs.

It is my wish that these 10 keys will assist you in unlocking the magnificence that is just below the surface of your earthly personality, and give you the edge you've always craved in your life. To get the most out of this book, first, read it and allow the concepts to sink into your mind. Next, use what you've learned. Make it a part of your daily practice to be conscious, to make different choices about what you think and believe, choosing only empowering thoughts and beliefs, and one day you will find that you are effortlessly Living a Soul Life.

Key 1 – Harness the Power of Your Own Mind

Before we can live a "Soul Life" and Create the Life We Desire and Deserve, I think it is important that we try to get an idea of what our Soul really is. The proverbial "Who are we?" question.

Soul: the immortal part of man, as distinguished from his body// the moral and emotional nature of man, as distinguished from his mind (or ego)// the vital principle which moves and animates all life. *Webster's Dictionary*

Here are some words others have used to describe "Soul":

Essence * Life Force * Spirit * Indwelling Spirit

Animating Force or Power * Divine Spark * Vital Force

Inspiriting Force (FYI "inspirit" is synonymous with "inspired")

Flame * Spark of Life * Vital Spirit * Consciousness * Life Essence

Divine Breath * Seat of Life * Essence of Life

To Put Life Into, to Invigorate * The Self * The Higher Self

The Spiritual One * The One * The God Within

The Essence Self * The Christ Within * The Angel

The Flame of Spirit * Director * The Observer

The Divine Perceiver * The Watcher * The Interpreter

Whichever of these words feels right to you, *is* right for you. It's all good. It is very difficult to label something in human terms that is beyond our understanding in the form we inhabit currently on the earth plane. We are the essence or divine spark of God living in a human body. We are more powerful than we even know.

As Jesus said, “"If you have faith as small as a mustard seed, you can say to this mulberry tree, 'Be uprooted and planted in the sea,' and it will obey you.” Luke 17:6

If we understood how powerful our mind and beliefs are we could access all the forces of the universe and literally move mountains. We have forgotten who we are. It is my hope that by helping you understand how your mind works, you will have the tools necessary to begin the process of remembering.

The first key and probably the most important thing to know is key number 1 - harness the power of your own mind by understanding your own consciousness.

Following is a psychological model of the mind. Experts agree, we use less than 5% of our mind at a conscious level. That leaves over 95% of our consciousness that is below the surface or subconscious.

Your conscious mind is your wide-awake mind, it is the reasoning, rational, logical mind. This is where you do all your critical thinking. And it loves to believe it’s in control.

Did you ever stick to your New Year's Resolutions? If you're anything like most people, the New Year's Resolutions were out the door by February if not sooner. There is a reason for this.

Incidentally, in this 5% conscious level, this is where your will power is. And probably, most importantly, this is where your ego is. So, if your subconscious mind is not in alignment with your conscious, ego driven goals, it's like running into a brick wall over and over again, and you have to work very hard to achieve even the slightest success.

To follow are 2 diagrams that represent the subconscious and conscious minds. The pluses and minuses in the subconscious mind model represent all of your memories and experiences stored there. The parentheses represent those experiences that have a powerful emotional energy attached to them, which make them impactful.

The subconscious mind is below the surface of our conscious awareness and is the gateway to higher aspects of our consciousness or superconscious, divine connection.

Although the subconscious is always aware and responding to our thoughts and feelings, the most effective way to make a higher connection is through meditation, intention, and quieting the conscious/ego mind chatter.

The conscious/ego mind appears as the "real" you, but is really a tiny fragment of your true essence. The conscious mind or ego thrives on drama and is very manipulative in its need for superficial gratification. When unconscious about this aspect, we can find ourselves efforting for every little thing, out of flow with the world and dissatisfied, possibly creating disharmony, even in our bodies.

It is through our conscious awakening to this illusion, the illusion of egoic thinking and behaving, that we begin the process of accessing deeper, higher, more profound and enlightened energies and ways of being.

True joy will come effortlessly as we expand our awareness and access the hidden and powerful recesses of our unlimited subconscious. During this process, as our vibratory energy rasies, we find infinite potential, abundance and joy is already ours and is our divine birthright!

Please review the following diagrams.

The Mind Model

Subconscious: >95% Below the surface. All Memories,

Emotions, Habits (conditioned responses),

Imagination, Learns very quickly, Number One Priority to Protect.

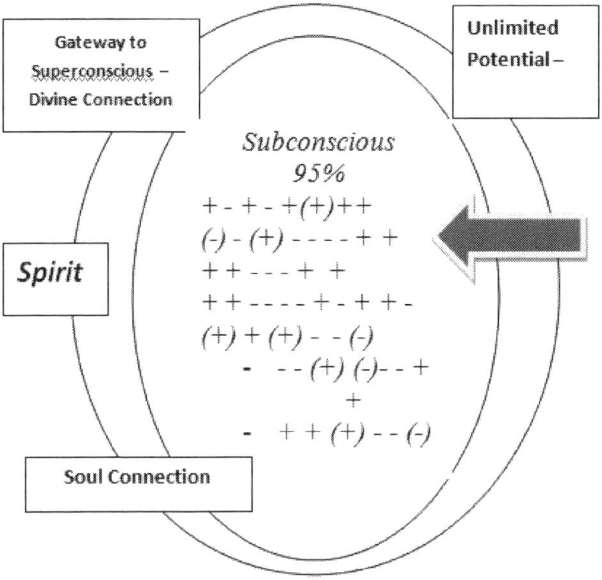

Conscious Mind

(Outer Ring – On the Surface)

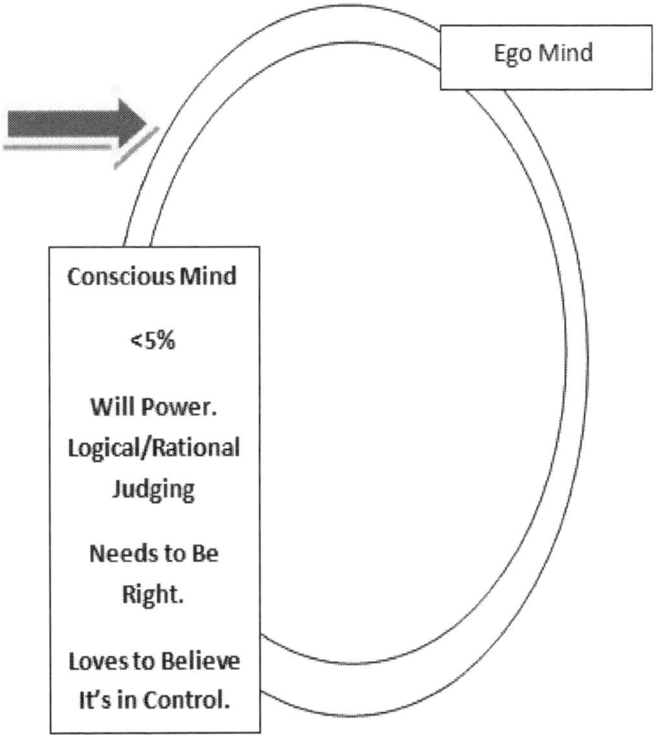

Here are some things you might want to know about the ego so you can recognize when you are experiencing life from that point of view.

- The ego judges everything and is very critical of you and others.
- The ego demands its own way.
- The ego has to be right.
- The ego is never satisfied.
- The ego is in the illusion that it has control of circumstances and often, other people.
- The ego is easily offended.
- The ego will create drama in order to substantiate its existence and importance.

So if you find yourself feeling offended, or in an argument where you need to be right, or you're judging others or yourself, and when you don't feel good enough, then it's safe to say, you're probably operating from this conscious aspect of the ego.

What does this all add up to?:

STRESS

Do you feel joyful when you're stressed?

Probably not.

Have you ever really thought about it? Stress doesn't really exist. It's a completely man-made concept. You can't touch it, you can't bottle it. It is a complete by-product of our thinking. The good news is…that means we can change it.

Just to be fair, I thought I should look up ego in the dictionary too.

Webster's Dictionary defines the ego:

A term to describe the "I", the subject of which is conscious of itself, thinks, has experience of and determines the outside world// the individual self, looked on as an organized being distinct from others, one's image of oneself; the conscious personality as opposed to the unconscious.

So, unlike the Soul, the ego, is separate from everyone and everything and it's very self-centered. The ego is a part of us that is like a small child that wants its own way and is never satisfied. Nothing, including itself is ever good enough. Once this part of you has something it wanted, it usually wants something else. Have you ever noticed that?

There may be some "thing" that you just have to have. The ego can nag at you and create the feeling that you can't live without "it." The ego makes you believe that having this "thing" will make you feel good about yourself, your friends will be jealous, etc. But once you finally get it, the excitement is over almost immediately or short lived.

Operating from ego consciousness is very, very frustrating. Not only to everyone outside of you, but to yourself. It doesn't feel good to never be satisfied or feel good enough. It reminds me of the Rolling Stone's song: *"I can't get no satisfaction. Hey, hey, hey!"*

But, there is good news.

When you bcome aware of this aspect of you more of the time – you can change it.

Let's talk a little bit about the subconscious, the over 95% of your consciousness.

We can use the terms "unconscious" and "subconscious" interchangeably, but I think unconscious sends the wrong idea. Truthfully, we are never really unconscious, because there's always an aspect of our consciousness, below the surface, that is aware and working. So I like to refer to this level of consciousness as the subconscious for our purposes here.

The first thing that is really important to understand is that your subconscious mind is the part of you that runs all of your body functions. Everything taking place in your body right now is happening automatically and below the surface of your conscious awareness. Your heart is beating, your food is digesting, pupils dilating at the precise moment necessary, hormones and biochemicals, brain chemicals are constantly balancing and rejuvenating, muscles are firing, cells are renewing themselves and old cells are dying off, as your body is eliminating them. When you take a walk or go up the stairs, your heart rate and breathing adjust automatically. You don't have to consciously tell your eyes to blink or your skin to tan. Millions of physical, and biochemical functions are all happening, right now and you don't even have to think about it.

The number 1 priority of the subsconscious is to protect and keep you from harm, physically, mentally and emotionally. Due to this "primary function" there is an innate intelligence within you that knows how to heal you and keep you healthy, safe and alive.

What happens when you cut your finger? Why does it bleed?

The same for when you break your leg. This consciousness, this innate intelligence within you, sends immediate healing, and in some cases pain killers, which flow through your blood. I'm not a medical doctor or a biologist so in no way can I get technical here, but you get the idea. The healing intelligence, which is innate within you, is always there, immediately and always working to keep you healthy, safe and alive.

If you were to step off a curb and a bus was barreling down upon you, you'd automatically step back onto the curb. You don't even think about it, you react. That is a function of the subconscious mind. What's really important to understand is that this consciousness is in every cell in your body and every cell is in instantaneous communication with the other cells. This consciousness is within and all around you.

We can begin to see this mind/body connection.

This same intelligence also protects you from emotional harm or pain. It is in the subconscious where all your memories and experiences are stored, all your emotions, habit patterns or conditioned responses. This part of your consciousness is very much like a computer. Except, unlike a computer, the subconscious has unlimited storage, it has infinity megabytes.

Looking at the Mind Model, the pluses and minuses represent your experiences and your particular perception of those experiences as good or bad, based on your individual personality, family belief structure, decision making process and thoughts from the conscious mind.

Your subconscious has been storing all of your experiences, whether you were consciously aware of them or not, since the moment you became a consciousness. I'll let you absorb that for a moment. Since we are made of energy and energy never dies, only transforms…potentially you've been a consciousness forever.

The subconscious learns very quickly and can make a life altering change in a moment.

Unlike a computer, each of us is unique. Although we are alike, not one of us is exactly the same. We're more like snowflakes. Each of us will learn and grow in the way that is perfect for us as individuals and that benefits the collective whole. Our beliefs and subconscious programs will feedback to us and manifest themselves uniquely for each of us based on the many factors of our personality, upbringing and primarily our perceptions of every experience. Just like snowflakes, not one of us is exactly alike in our perceptions.

Probably, the most important thing I'm going to say to you is this:

The subconscious mind does not know the difference between what's real and what you imagine. Your imagination is your most powerful tool, physically, mentally, emotionally *and* spiritually. Anything you can imagine, you can create.

Let's explore why this is so.

The subconscious mind does not judge anything. In simple terms, it gets directions from your conscious thoughts and beliefs, simultaneously scans all the experiences stored in the subconscious level to find support for those thoughts and beliefs, then provides that supporting information as feedback to your conscious mind. Thereby reinforcing what you're thinking about or imagining. So whatever you're thinking about or imagining will become true for you.

Your thoughts and beliefs create your reality, literally. (We will explore the power of your imagination in more detail in Key 3.)

For example: Let's say you're thinking: "Why does this always happen to me?" The subconscious mind registers the thought and begins to do a data search through your memories and experiences or subconscious programs and brings up, to the surface, all those experiences that support that thought.

What if you were to think to yourself: "I am so organized. I always get the job done."

Again, the subconscious mind registers the thought and begins to search through your memories and beliefs to bring up all those experiences which support *that* thought, thereby reinforcing the thought or belief that you are indeed organzed and get things done.

It doesn't really matter to the subconscious mind what you're thinking about, whatever you're thinking about, you're being supported. Unlike the ego in the conscious level of the mind, the subconscious mind is non-judgmental.

It's so important to understand this and learn how to harness this wonderful power that is you and get it working for you instead of against you. When you become aware of how your thoughts are affecting how you feel, you can choose to think more empowering thoughts. Remaining unconscious to this process keeps you stuck in a victim mentality, reacting to the circumstances outside of you, basically thinking the same thoughts over and over again, and working against yourself.

Key 2 – Your Thoughts Create Your Reality

Why Do I Feel Like This?

All emotion follows thought.

One of the predominant shifts that have been happening in the so-called "New Age" movement of the last 25 years, is the growing belief that you create your own reality. Your words or thoughts create what you say and think about. This is absolutely true because all emotion follows thought, so your words and thoughts create emotions. The subconscious mind provides feedback from your stored experiences, you then experience feelings that are references in the subconscious mind. You can't feel anything if you didn't think it first or if you have never experienced the feeling before.

Have you ever noticed that children, for the most part seem naturally happy. It is the beliefs and energy of parents and caretakers that spill over into children which can begin the process of shutting down their joy. We must be very careful to allow children to maintain their innocence and wonderment.

To begin to live a Soul Life, a life of joy and wellness, success and right relationship, we have to get a handle on our own thinking. To do this we have to become aware of what we're thinking about and what we're saying.

It's estimated that during the average day, a human thinks over 75,000 thoughts. Stay tuned, because you'll probably think the same thoughts again tomorrow.

Talk about stress.

To alleviate stress and to be able to a soul-filled life, we have to quiet these thoughts down and take charge of what we're thinking about. Thoughts become habits and we can create new habits, it just takes awareness and practice.

The best way to begin a practice of monitoring your thoughts is to tune into and be aware of your emotions. Be aware of those times when you don't feel as good as you would like. Be aware of those times when you feel great. Notice what you are thinking about and you will know what initiated the feeling. Once you are aware, you can change the thoughts accordingly to something that feels better. Or, if you're feeling great, you can utilize the empowering sequence of the current thoughts to shift your feelings at a lower emotional time.

Stop, take a moment, get quiet and tune in. Observe your thoughts and then notice where the emotion is located in your body. This will tell you a great deal about how the issue is affecting you physically and how it is influencing your energy systems.

Each place in your body is connected with an energy system that has a meaning connected to what you're feeling.

For example, a gut feeling may mean you're being affected in your solar plexes or power center. Tightness in your chest may mean, your heart is involved and you're not feeling loved and supported. Tightness in your throat area may mean you are not speaking your truth or that the issue revolves around a lie. You can learn more about this by reading about Chakras, which is beyond the scope of this book.

After you've become aware of the feeling and where you're experiencing it in your body, next ask yourself: What was I just thinking about?

This is a good place to start. To be most effective at this we're going to do a short meditation and learn to use the power of your breath. Focusing on your breath will allow your nervous system to relax and help you to quiet your mind and become fully present in the moment.

So let's get started in the process of harnessing the power of our thoughts.

The most wonderful thing about this is that it's relaxing. And not only are we learning how to use the power of our thoughts to create a wonderful life, (a little secret here ☺) when we meditate and quiet down the thoughts of the ego, we give our nervous system a break from the pressure of our personality. That release of pressure allows our innate connection with our Higher Self, our Soul consciousness. It is this connection that raises our vibration or frequency and takes us to a place of inner peace and tranquility. In other words, as we raise our energy vibration, we release stress and transcend any issues we may be experiencing in our daily lives. In addition, it has been proven that meditation releases powerful brain chemicals of happiness, like endorphens. This automatically makes you feel better.

So, let's get comfortable.

We're going to take the first steps with our first meditation to quieting our mind and monitoring our thoughts. (if you've ordered this by ebook, you've received a free audio meditation – to go with this.) You may purchase the audio on my site http://www.suziebowers.com.

Your breath is the key to getting into the correct state to be effective with this. So let's practice breathing.

Breath is the key

Take a deep breath in and exhale.

Doesn't that feel good?

Notice your breath. Were you holding it? Are you breathing deeply or shallowly?

Now, take a deep breath in through your nose and release through your mouth.

Blow the air out in a nice, even, steady stream.

Inhale again, deeply, and intend to relax as you exhale.

Observe how you feel.

Place your hand on your belly, somewhere around your navel.

Breathe deeply in through your nose and bring the air down into your belly. Imagine your belly is like a balloon and you're filling it with air. Hold it. Count one-thousand-one, one-thousand-two and exhale, blowing the air out again in an even steady stream out your mouth.

Using your diaphragm, push all the remaining air out of your belly, out of your lungs, and hold it now at the bottom of the breath, count one-thousand-one, one-thousand-two and inhale.

Inhaling through your nose, bringing the air down into your belly. Now bringing your awareness into the center of your being. Feel yourself anchoring into the center of your body. Good. Hold it, one-thousand-one, one-thousand-two, and exhale, blowing it out

again in an even steady stream until you've gently pushed all the air out.

Repeat the process 5 or 6 times and then let your breathing relax.

Please relax and breathe at your own pace, (after 5 or 6 breaths.)

As you allow your breathing to relax to your normal, natural breathing rhythm observe your body.

How do you feel?

Next step. Bring your awareness to your nostrils now, with your eyes gently closed. Follow your breath in and out, imagine you can see it in your mind's eye, flowing gently in and out of your nose. Feel it flowing in and out, as well.

Now, observe your mind. Compared to your normal daily thinking are you having a lot of thoughts or a few thoughts? Observe the thoughts as they come up or drift by. You are the observer, not the thinker. When you catch yourself becoming the

thinker and getting involved in the thoughts, bring your awareness back to your breath. Follow the breath in and out, in and out.

And again, observe the thoughts.

You can tell when you become the thinker of the thoughts when one thought leads into another and another. Usually, you're thinking of things you need to do next or tomorrow. You may have thoughts that are judging, such as, is this really working, does she know what she's talking about? That's the ego and that's you returning to the conscious level and once again becoming "unconscious." Recognize it, without judgment, from this wiser, quieter, perspective of your Soul. If you can't stay with being the observer then bring the awareness back to your breath.

Keep practicing until it gets easy to slow down the mind. This is how we become conscious in the present moment.

It is in this space of quieting the thoughts where we can access the powerful subconscious mind level, where we can make changes to the way we think and feel about ourselves, our past and the world around us. It is in this state of quiet connection where affirmations are most powerful. Choose a few affirmations in advance and then say them to yourself in this relaxed and quiet place.

Affirmations are a great way to change your thought patterns and can be used any time. However, dropping them in after creating stillness in the conscious mind is extremely powerful and will have the most and lasting impact. (I have provided some some helpful affirmations at the end of this book, to help get you started.)

Now, take one final cleansing breath and come back into full awareness. Come back into the room, allow your eyes to open and come back feeling very refreshed and revitalized and focused.

How does that feel?

Now just like anything, this takes practice.

The steps are:

1. Several deep breaths, getting the breath down low in the body.
2. Imagine you're blowing up your belly balloon.

3. Hold the breath 1, 2.
4. Exhale through the mouth, blowing the air out in an even steady stream.
5. Hold 1, 2 and
6. Again inhale through your nose, and hold.
7. After 5 or 6 breaths or once you've relaxed, allow your breathing to return to your natural rhythm. Observe your breath as you follow it in and out.
8. Observe the thoughts.
9. When you catch yourself thinking, bring the awareness back to your breath.
10. Repeat the process
11. Recognize and observe the ego thinking, judging, planning, questioning, rationalizing, etc.
12. Breathe and drop in a positive affirmation.

Remember, for affirmations to be most powerful, we must speak the language of the subconscious mind. Affirmations must be spoken in the positive and as if they were true now.

Keep out words like *don't*. For example:

Wrong: I don't want to overeat anymore.
Correct: I release the need to overeat from this point forward.

Wrong: I don't want to feel bad anymore.
Correct: I am healthy, alive and filled with joy.

Wrong: I can't afford it.
Correct: Financial success comes to me now.

So this is the beginning step to becoming conscious of what is going on below the surface. Remember: emotion follows thought.

If you're not feeling as good as you would like, you have to change your thoughts. You have to change your focus, eliminate negative thinking and speak the language of the subconscious mind.

One final tip: exercise will assist you in changing your state of mind too, after which, will give you a better base to start your thought monitoring process. Since the mind and body are one, physical movements will create a new state of mind as well. Exercise not only relieves stress and increases blood flow, but also releases powerful biochemicals like endorphins, which make us feel good.

Key 3 – Beliefs

"Anything that affects our thinking affects our lives. And nothing else affects our thinking more than our beliefs."

Infinite Possibilities, The Art of Living Your Dreams. Mike Dooley

During the young years of our earthly life we are influenced greatly by our family's values. Their beliefs become our beliefs and as we have life experiences, more beliefs begin to develop and create the filter with which we view the world.

Beliefs are given to us, from our parents, our grandparents, our siblings, from our society, from religion and teachers, even the media plays a part. Beliefs give us comfort through the scary night. Since we are creatures of habit and fear what we do not understand, beliefs can feel comfortable, even when they're not good for us. They give us a sense of connection with our family, of belonging to our tribe. Even if our family experience wasn't that great, in a pinch we will still fall back into the comfort zone of our family's belief system because it's familiar. You can often get a clear picture of your beliefs by listening to what you say.

Have you ever had the experience when you were angry with one of your kids or with your significant other, of hearing your mother's voice come out of your mouth? Well I certainly have. I swore I would never do things the way Mom did because I am so much smarter than she. (Laugh out loud.) Yet, in a moment of frustration or even panic, subconscious programs and beliefs will bubble up to the surface for instant reference.

The subconscious mind records and stores every experience you've ever had since the moment you became a consciousness, so it is all in there.* In addition to our family beliefs, all of our own experiences form into our own set of unique beliefs about the world, how things work and how we fit into the puzzle called life.

* (Since we are energy and energy can never die, only transform, we must conclude that we have been a consciousness for all time.)

Whatever you focus on, you get more of. That is a function of the subconscious mind, but it is the ego that wants to be right, so it will find references out in the world that make our beliefs true for us. This can be in the form of other people or groups that have the same or similar beliefs as we do.

The problem is that most beliefs are false and keep us stuck from opening our mind to the unlimited potential that *is* us and is available to us.

Beliefs that are held in the subconscious mind can hold us back and keep us from experiencing life to the fullest level of our unlimited potential. Some beliefs can keep us from experiencing the unlimited joy and love that is available to us at all times.

To truly live a spiritually based life, full of joy and prosperity, which is based on growth and learning, we must begin to recognize and unravel our beliefs.

While I was attending a spiritual retreat last weekend, the topic of beliefs came up. And we discussed how our beliefs hold us back and feed our ego. The ego is the part of us that holds us back from joy and success in life.

Remember, the ego creates drama and needs to be right in order to substantiate its existence. It is the part of us that feeds on controversy. Ego identification can create a firm hold with our beliefs, and this will never lead to happiness. It is that simple.

Think how wonderful our whole world would be if we weren't fighting over everyone's beliefs, who is right and who is wrong. Everywhere in the world, different people have different sets of beliefs based on their history and past conditioning. You may be here in the U.S. and have a completely different set of beliefs than someone who grew up in Africa, Asia or the Middle East. Every group of people, every person has their own experience of family, of society, of religion and every person is susceptible to those belief systems that were ingrained into them. Does that really make them wrong, because their ideas or concepts of life differ from ours?

Truth is, even in the U.S. and Canada, from one region to another, we have differing belief systems.

I want to tell you a funny story I heard years ago. I'm definitely paraphrasing here:

There was a woman, we'll call her Harriet. Well Harriet invited me to dinner one night and as she put the roast on she cut off one side of it. I asked her, "Harriet, why did you just cut off that side of the roast?"

She told me because that's how she'd always done it. "That's just how it's done." She said.

Her mother always cut off one side of the roast before she cooked it. Well come to find out, her mother did the same thing and her grandmother. We didn't know the reason why. I certainly do not cut a side of a roast off before cooking it. It didn't make any sense to me at all.

Then one day, we were talking about this in front of her grandmother and she just started laughing. "What?" we asked her. She told us the reason she cut off a side of the roast was because the only pan she had wasn't big enough to hold the whole roast, so she always had to cut off one side to make it fit.

This story is funny, but the point is that it illustrates how beliefs can be so ingrained into us that we don't take a minute to question them and make sure it really fits for us now.

It's a challenge to be open-minded when we're so sure that we know what we know. I've had friends who claim to be "born again Christians" and are so certain that they know.

Yet, there is a plethora of evidence to show that there are other truths and documents, other people's experiences and other pathways that to someone else are just as valid. I could sit there and show them the proof in black and white and they still would dismiss it as "not the way" and stay stuck in this one way of seeing things. This is a sure way to miss out on infinite amounts of wisdom and knowledge that would otherwise make life richer and more complete.

There is no God that uses hate and violence to enforce a belief in one path or another. Any group or individual using violence, shame or hate to persuade another is not operating from God Consciousness, which is only love and acceptance. Any entity that uses the tactic "persuade others" is coming from pure ego consciousness and has the need to be right. This is the antithesis of Soul Consciousness and should be avoided at all costs.

Certainly it is more comfortable to know what you know and stick with it. It really sucks to be wrong when you're living from ego consciousness.

I am not putting down Christians or any other spiritual tradition and truly many religions claim to be "the only way." This is just one example of how people can be very self-righteous and stubborn about a belief that may or may not be valid in reality. I like to use this example because I think we can all relate to it.

Years ago, I even had a well-meaning friend tell me at lunch one day, while she was sipping her glass of wine, that I was going to "hell" if I didn't accept Jesus Christ as my savior and as God. Maybe you have had a similar experience. I just cannot figure out how so much judgment of others could possibly be "Christian," or spiritually based. There are 6 billion people on this planet with many different spiritual beliefs and experiences. How could only one path lead to God, the Father/Mother of All That Is?

Our entire Universe and everything beyond is pure energy and we are all part of that same energy, right down to a grain of sand and a blade of grass. We are made from the same stuff as the stars, each and every one of us. Every being is a divine spark of the Great Spirit that moves, creates and animates all life, none better or more worthy than another regardless of outside appearances.

Regardless of what spiritual path you choose to go down, if any, my point is to elevate your awareness to the thought, the possibility that there is so much you do not know. And the only way to find out is to keep a receptive and open-minded attitude. Be aware of what may in fact be a belief and not something that is valid and may not be serving you today in your quest for joy and success. You may be amazed, as I have been, by the levels of awareness and awe you can experience when you set aside what you think you know and open to the infinite possibilities that are available to us. As unlimited energy beings, we are capable of experience multiple dimensions of reality that until that moment you shifted your beliefs, were invisible to you.

Becoming conscious of your unconscious beliefs is an extremely important element in accepting responsibility for every area of your life. You will not move forward until you examine each and every belief that comes up.

How will you know when a belief has come up?

It is the same process of being aware of our thoughts and feelings. The moment you recognize you are having some emotion about a situation or another person, when you find yourself "upset," it is time to stop, breathe and make a conscious decision to go one step back and take a serious look at yourself.

Get quiet, breathe deeply, relax and focus on your breath, quieting the "ego mind."

Observe what ***you*** are thinking about, not how the other person is wrong or how *they* made you feel. If you catch yourself going into internal dialogue, rehearsing the conversation over again, or how the other person is wrong, you are back into "ego mind," so you want to again bring your attention back to your breath. Follow your breath in and out your nostrils, until your thoughts quiet down. Observe what you're thinking about the situation. Remember, all emotion follows thought, so that's where to begin.

Next, ask yourself these questions:

- What belief or perception within myself is causing this emotional reaction within me?
- Where are these thoughts coming from?
- Am I accepting responsibility for my emotional state?

- Do I choose to be upset about this situation or am I on subconscious auto-pilot, reacting instead of observing?
- Is what being said directed at me or could the other person mean something entirely different than what I am thinking and perceiving?
- What belief(s) do I need to examine and possibly change?
- What is it I am here to learn from this experience?

These questions are a good start and may begin a series of deeper questions that will assist you in re-centering and perhaps in choosing a different more empowering response where everyone can win. Remember, when you come from the perspective of the Observer…your Soul-self, you will diffuse any offensive energies within you, which will allow you to view the situation from a higher more loving level. Stay in your heart as you Observe. Stay out of your ego.

Beliefs can affect every area of our lives.

We can have beliefs about money, relationships, health, animals, the environment, education, politics, religion, sex, the weather, you name it. And each belief has the ability to keep us stuck in mediocrity, sickness, poverty and despair. Conversely, beliefs can also empower us and move us forward with enthusiasm and a zest for life, regardless of outer circumstances.

Which do you choose? It is a choice.

As you get better at recognizing your disempowering beliefs, you can change them by saying "cancel clear," and instead pop in an empowering affirmation.

For example: "I am so disgusted with myself, I'm too fat. I shouldn't have eaten that piece of pie."

"Cancel/Clear!" (This wipes out the previous thought.)

Affirm: "Everything I eat metabolizes perfectly so I maintain my healthy weight around 145 lbs."

Example 2: "I can't afford that."

"Cancel/Clear!"

Affirm: "An unlimited flow of abundance and money come to me now."

This is a powerful way to use affirmations to shift negative thinking and therefore assist us in creating new more empowering beliefs.

How you choose to think and feel and what you choose to believe is your choice. Decide today that you will feel joyful under any and all circumstances by accepting responsibility for your own mind and how you use it. If a situation presents itself where you find you are not feeling as joyful or as good as you would like, be grateful that you have another opportunity to take a look at the underlying belief(s) and make a conscious decision to change it into something more empowering. Every time you get angry, depressed, or feel resentful you get another opportunity to grow and evolve into an even better you.

From the Soul's perspective, each person that you attract into your life is mutually there to assist each of you on your life journey, to evolve and grow. As you operate in your daily life as an awakened consciousness, no longer reacting to unconscious drama, or blaming others for your feelings and experience, you will begin to appreciate each person for the interactions they bring to you. These interactions give you that opportunity to clear out limiting beliefs. Even the most challenging relationships are gifts, given to us by our Higher Selves or Souls, to help us grow and raise our vibration to a higher level. So the next time someone makes you angry, or hurts your feelings, causes you to get offended, stop, step back and give gratitude for the lesson you are about to learn because of them. Thank them for holding a mirror up for you. It is truly a gift.

Your Beliefs and the Reticular Activating System

Now, we have discussed levels of consciousness as it pertains to the essence of day to day living, the conscious mind, (ego mind) which equates to less than 5% of our consciousness and the subconscious mind level, over 95% of our consciousness which lives within every cell of our body and beyond our physical selves. All our experiences are stored in the subconscious level which includes all our past emotions. The subconscious represents the gateway to the "superconscious" level, infinite connected consciousness, where our connection to our Soul and All That Is, Ever Was and Ever Will Be exists without time and without space.

The Reticular Activating System – Our Mind's Filtering Process

This may all sound a little cosmic or "New Age," but the truth is it fits perfectly with what we know about the physiology of the body and particularly the brain. Scientists have studied a part of our brain, about the size of the tip of your pinky finger, located at the base and within the brain which according to Wikipedia is an area (including the reticular formation and its connections) responsible for regulating arousal and sleep-wake transitions. In our terms, conscious level (5%) our wide-awake consciousness, "sleep" or below the surface, (95%) subconscious. It is called the RAS or Reticular Activating System.

Think of the RAS as a filtering system that allows in and filters out information.

Let's talk again about Beliefs before we connect the role of the RAS in determining what we experience.

What is a belief? As we discussed earlier, a belief is a conviction or a sense of certainty that something is true and leaves no room for doubt.

"Dictionary.com":
confidence in the truth or existence of something not immediately susceptible to rigorous proof.

Or Webster's Dictionary: *a state or habit of mind in which trust or confidence is placed in some person or thing. something believed; especially **:** a tenet or body of tenets held by a group or conviction of the truth of some statement or the reality of some being or phenomenon especially when based on examination of evidence.*

How do we continue to create beliefs?

In essence a belief starts out as an idea. The only difference between an idea and a belief is based on the amount or quantity (and sometimes quality) of references that they have. References are equivalent to experience or observation. The more experience, the more the idea weighs in on the side of belief.

A belief starts out as an idea. In the following example, let's plant a seed or an idea in the ground, deep in the subconscious mind. Every time we have an experience or reference that pertains to this idea, we begin to grow roots. Roots are references. The more roots or references we experience that become deeply entrained into the subconscious, the more powerful energy is born to create a belief.

As this belief grows and reaches for the light of our conscious awareness, it finally becomes the fruit or the "result" of the belief or original idea. Plant the seed in the subconscious, the tree, the leaves are the "fruit" or the results of that belief that show up in our day to day lives and continue to create our experience.

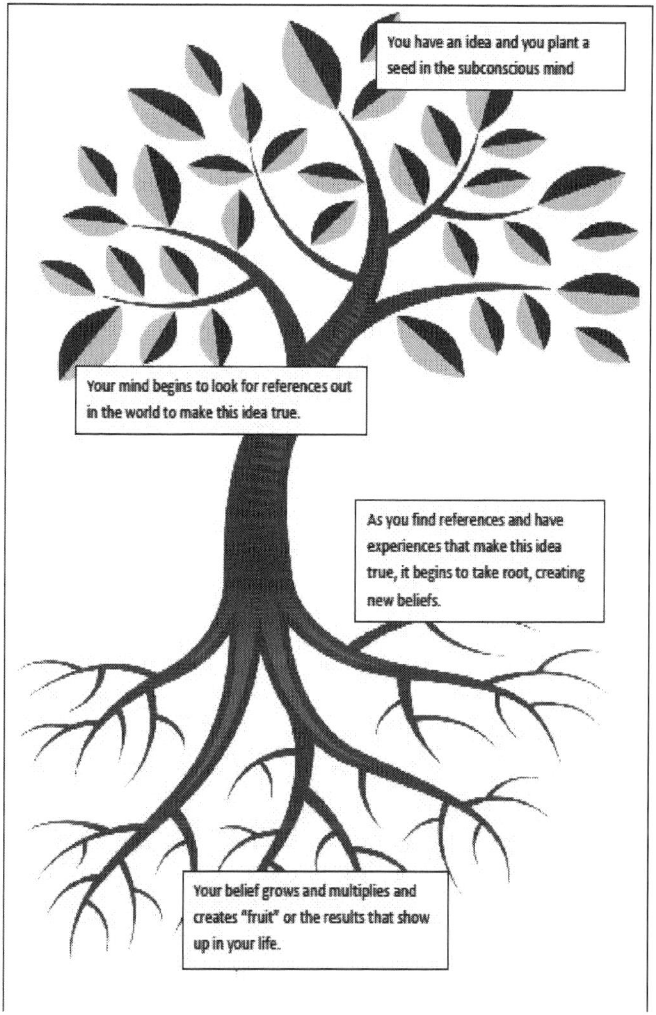
You have an idea and you plant a seed in the subconscious mind
Your mind begins to look for references out in the world to make this idea true.
As you find references and have experiences that make this idea true, it begins to take root, creating new beliefs.
Your belief grows and multiplies and creates "fruit" or the results that show up in your life.

Ideas planted in the subconscious mind will take root as we find references in our world to support them.

According to visionary, James Ray and co-founder of ViSalus Sciences, Blake Mallen, at any given time there are over 2 million bits of sensory data available to the human brain and to our consciousness to choose from. The maximum that the human nervous system can allow is 134 bits per second. So although we can only filter in a maximum of 134 bits of sensory data per second, our nervous system is being bombarded by over 2 million bits.

However, according to the experts in brain morphology, study of the brain, we only allow in between 5 and 9 bits of information at one time.

In essence, we are missing a huge amount of information. Truly we have no idea how the world works, because we are missing a gigantic amount of sensory data.

So what determines what you are letting into your subconscious?

The answer is: your brain, specifically the Reticular Activating System or RAS. The RAS only allows in what you tell it is important based on what? Based on your beliefs. Therefore, if you believe the world is a vicious, hostile, mean, nasty, selfish, unhappy, ugly place to live, you will find references that will make that true for you.

If you believe that the world is kind, supportive, loving, caring, abundant, and beautiful, you will find references that will make *that* true for you. Again, the choice is yours.

What about the things we say to ourselves? For example: what about the idea, "I am ____________." Or "I am not _____________?"

For example: "I am stupid or I am not worthy of prosperity/love/success/health/kindness/friends/happiness." (the list goes on, doesn't it.)

And of course, what about the things others say to us that we let in? Well meaning parents, teachers, relatives, sports authorities and significant others can often say very degrading and critical things to us that can hurt and create additional references and ultimately beliefs that dis-empower us. These authority figures in our lives may also behave in a certain way that allows beliefs to take hold of us at a subconscious level, giving us permission to also behave in a certain way even though it may be harmful to us. Again, though, we will only create beliefs regarding these words and deeds if we have references to support the idea.

For example, some of my beliefs about the world came from my father. Sometimes I would ask him for money to go to the store or for fun money and he would say things like, "money doesn't grow on trees." (I know you've heard that one.) Being native American, in the mid-west, my father grew up very poor. Interestingly, whenever my father would begin to achieve a level of success, which he did many times, he would always find a way to sabotage himself, by behaving badly, not showing up for work and at one point, actually stealing.

Dad was amazingly talented, people loved him. He had a genius IQ and an amazing gift for making people feel important. He was always given opportunities for further achievement, that many only dream of, even world travel. Yet, he would destroy his success every single time. He obviously had many references and beliefs that kept him stuck in poverty consciousness.

Conversely, my mother made good money, always worked, but she grew up in a well-to-do, country club atmosphere and she would hand me money any time I asked, as if there was always plenty to go around. She worked hard and had beliefs that encouraged her to blaze a trail into higher level management and a 6-figure income. No other women in her company had achieved this, at that time. Ironically, my mother ultimately made way more money than my father did and achieved huge success.

It is so important that we each take a serious look at what we "believe" to be true. If you are not experiencing all the joy, support and success you desire, then there are underlying beliefs that are keeping you stuck. Also, if you continue to attract unpleasant experiences, it is the underlying beliefs that are creating them. If something isn't working for you, change it. Obviously, there is so much more experience to be had than you have been conditioned to believe.

"To master your thoughts and imagination, and therefore your life and destiny, you must first master their captain-your beliefs."

Mike Dooley

Nothing is missing in our world. Everything, all experience is here and your experience will be based on what you tell your RAS is important. What you give attention to will grow and expand within you, attracting more of the same. The subconscious mind is a willing servant and will continue to look for references, aka "experiences" to make your beliefs true for you.

Aha! I hope that by now a light bulb is going off in your brain!

We all have the exact same opportunity to allow in any number of experiences within the 2 million bits of sensory data. Decide to be happy…decide to be sad, prosperous or poor, sick or healthy. What do you choose?

"For verily I say unto you, That whosoever shall say unto this mountain, Be thou removed, and be thou cast into the sea; and shall not doubt in his heart, but shall

believe that those things which he saith shall come to pass; he shall have whatsoever he saith." *Mark 11:23*

Belief Can Move Mountains

If you desire something different for yourself, change will require that you create new beliefs. You must be willing to question your beliefs about everything and again, the first step is to be aware of when you are not feeling as good as you would like, or recognize whenever you become offended. If you continue to leave your beliefs "unchecked", they can and will hold you hostage throughout your life. Question your beliefs when things are not going the way you'd like.

Could it be that your beliefs are keeping you from achieving happiness, prosperity or loving relationships?

Are your beliefs about health keeping you sick? What do you believe about relationships? Are you afraid to love and be loved. Is something holding you back?

You must believe that you deserve prosperity and abundance, love, and good health. Your subconscious mind will then find references to make it true for you. Your beliefs create your experience and attract to you more experiences to make your beliefs true. To create the life you desire and deserve, you must be willing to change your beliefs. Your beliefs either empower you or they suck the life out of you. Beliefs either assist you in living immersed in the joy of your Soul-self, or keep you disconnected and burdened.

Becoming aware of and examining our beliefs is a very important process in becoming conscious. Decide today that you will not allow yourself to feel from an unconscious level any further. Decide today to examine your experience and choose what is empowering, choose what feels good.

Key 4-The Power of Your Imagination

The subconscious mind does not know the difference between what's real and what you imagine.

Think on this for just a moment. There is incredible power within your inherent right to imagine and daydream.

I'd like to give you some examples. If were to say to you right now, I want you to recall or imagine a time when you felt very, very sad. Perhaps, a time when you lost someone, maybe your dog or favorite pet, maybe a friend or loved one. Just by thinking about this sad time, you can feel sad very easily.

Take a deep breath and let that go. Now, I'd like you to think about and imagine a time when you felt really, really happy. This may be a special celebration, wedding, or anniversary or a time when you accomplished something and felt really proud of your accomplishment. Really remember it as if you were there. Close your eyes and see what you saw, feel what you felt, hear the sounds and recall the smells, really remember it.

That's right, makes you kind of want to smile inside and out.

Have you ever had the experience of hearing an old song on the radio that was popular when you were younger, maybe in high school, and you can remember the words and it reminds you of your old friends? We all have. All of your memories and experiences are stored in the subconscious mind and this kind of recall is directly connected to our power of imagination.

Typically imagination correlates with your ability to create pictures in your mind and truly visualization is a very powerful tool. But it also relates to the other senses as well, because when a memory comes into your conscious awareness, it may have been triggered by a smell, a feeling, or something you have heard or seen.

I've had clients who have said to me, "I can't visualize or see pictures in my mind."

I always smile when I hear that because although, it's true that some people are better at creating pictures in their mind, everyone can visualize.

If I were to say to you: "close your eyes and DO NOT under any circumstances see a 6 foot tall, white rabbit in a tuxedo wearing a black top hat and red cane, swigging a bottle of Jack Daniels."

What happens?

You really can't help yourself. You can get some sort of image in your mind of this 6 foot tall white rabbit in a tuxedo, wearing a black top hat and red cane. Maybe I can see it in more detail than you, because I am very visual, but you will get some sort of idea in your mind.

The incredible thing about this is that your subconscious mind doesn't know that it is "make believe." Everything that you imagine or create in your mind is registered by the subconscious as reality and it will begin to go to work to make that image real.

There is no time and space in the subconscious mind, everything is right now. As I pointed out before, by imagining past emotional experiences, you will begin to feel the emotions that you felt before. The subconscious mind responds perfectly to your every wish, or in this case every imagining, by providing the emotional feedback to what you're thinking of.

Your emotions are extremely important to this process. Emotions are the language of the subconscious mind. The stronger the emotion attached to your memory or what you're visualizing now, the more engaged the subconscious is in the process.

Why is this important?

If you are going to utilize the power of your imagination for creating and manifesting what you desire, then you will want to get your emotions involved and act as if you already have the thing or experience you desire. Remember, the subconscious mind's number 1 priority is to keep you happy, healthy, safe and alive.

While you visualize what you desire, allow yourself to feel deliriously happy and pretend you already have it. As your subconscious registers the joy you are feeling, it will access powerful forces within you and universal energy to create the desired result. These forces and energy are like powerful magnets, attracting all the circumstances and people to make the image held in your mind, your reality. Your imagination and subconscious are the gateways to unlimited, unmanifest potential and the collective consciousness where we are One Mind.

You might be asking right now, "well, how do I get myself to feel deliriously happy?"

Good question. It's easier than you think.

Begin by thinking of something else that makes you happy. For example, think of a cute little puppy. Or think about something else that makes you feel good, like when you accomplished something important or when someone acknowledged you. After you've gotten into a joyful state, try to maintain the feeling while you imagine receiving what you desire. Another fun trick, which was taught to me by a dear old friend and my Mary Lady, was to save all the thank you notes and cards you've ever received. Keep a special file and whenever you want to create a great feeling, get them out and read them. Read all the sweet things people have said to you. This will help you remember all the times when you did something special that touched someone else. These cards will evoke emotions in you, reminding you of how truly loved and cared for you are.

Physical exercise will also assist you in feeling good. Work out, sweat, walk, get silly, move your body, listen to your favorite music, dance and laugh.

Next, really see yourself in your life as if you already have this thing or experience. See it in detail, feel how it feels, smell the good smells, hear the fabulous sounds, all the things that make it real to you. The suconscious does not know whether this is real or not and will access its' unlimited resources to begin creating all the circumstances necessary for this to be.

Check this out. Your imagination, your thoughts and your words will cause changes in your physical body, whether you are aware of it or not.

Here's another little experiment I like to share when I'm speaking: Close your eyes and imagine you are standing in front of a lemon tree. Pick a ripe, juicy lemon from the tree and as you do a spray of lemon juice fills the air and your nostrils with a strong citrus, lemony fragrance.

Tear into that lemon with your hands and bring the bright yellow, dripping lemon up to your mouth and take a big suck. Mmmmmmm.

Ninety-five percent of the audience will have some sort of feeling or experience in their body, like having their mouth water, or actually being able to taste the lemon in their mouth.

Your imagination has a direct affect on your body and the world around you. As you can probably tell by now, if your mouth will water at imagining sucking on a lemon, then your imagination can also affect your body and heal it. Whether or not you experience your mouth watering, this is still true. The mind can heal the body and imagination and belief are the secret ingredients. We will discuss this further in the next chapter.

Another rule of the subconscious mind, is that if you can imagine it, and believe that you will have it, you *are capable of* achieving it. So imagine away. You really can create the life you desire and deserve. In a future key we will be discussing how our imagination, our thoughts and our feelings are energy and how our entire universe is manifested and unmanifested energy that responds to those thoughts.

In the Soul Plane, everything is unmanifest energy and pure potential. Your subconscious and your imagination are the doorways to bring *that* energy into the physical world. You are creator of your life and much more powerful than you even know.

"Follow Your Dreams; they're yours for a reason, not the least of which is to make them come true." Mike Dooley

Your imagination is the gateway to the "superconscious" mind level, where you have access to non-physical beings, other universes, past and future, and other dimensions. It is through the imagination that we can access the "collective mind" which is the Soul-level where we are all One energy. All knowledge is accessible through the power of your imagination.

Key 5 – The Mind and the Body Are Parallel Universes

***"Nothing takes place in the mind without leaving tracks in the body."* Deepak Chopra**

Earlier on I shared that your consciousness lives in every cell in your body. This is true. It has been scientifically proven that what we think about or imagine can have an immediate effect on our bodies.

Just ask, Dr. Denis Waitley, who applied the visualization process used by the Apollo space program to train Olympic athletes:

"When you visualize, then you materialize. We took Olympic athletes and had them run their event only in their mind, and then hooked them up to sophisticated biofeedback equipment. Incredibly, the same muscles fired in the same sequence when they were running the race in their mind as when they were running it on the track. How could this be? Because the mind can't distinguish whether you're really doing it or whether it's just a practice. If you've been there in the mind, you'll

go there in the body." Denis Waitley – from The Secret, Rhonda Byrne.

I heard of an experiment years ago that was conducted by the University of Toronto, Department of Psychology. They were testing the effects of visualization and imagination on the ability to shoot basketballs successfully into the hoop.

The experimenters created 3 groups.

1. A control group that did nothing.
2. A group that visualized making baskets for an hour a day.
3. A 3rd group that actually practiced shooting baskets for an hour each day.

The results were intriguing. After 30 days, as expected the control group showed no improvement. The group that practiced shooting baskets for an hour a day showed improvement and the group that only visualized shooting baskets showed the same if not better percentage of improvement than the group that actually practiced. The subconscious mind does not know the difference. What you imagine is not only real to your subconscious, it has a direct affect on your physical body.

In another study facilitated by the U.S. government, human DNA was extracted from a live donor. The donor's DNA was in another room being observed by powerful microscopes and measuring devices.

In a separate room, the DNA donor was shown various photos and movie clips designed to evoke powerful emotions. Whenever the donor experienced any emotion, the DNA registered a response at the exact same moment. The experimenters wanted to see if this would still be the case if they separated the donor and the DNA by distance. They stopped the experiment after concluding that the donor's emotions continued to effect the DNA 50 miles away with no lag time.

Other groups continued the experiment taking the DNA hundreds of miles away from the donor and achieved the exact same results. (You can find out more about this in The Divine Matrix, by Gregg Braden.)

We can conclude, our thoughts, our emotions and what we picture in our mind has a direct affect on our bodies. The mind and body *are* parallel universes. We can also conclude that our thoughts and emotions affect our bodies even when our DNA is far away from us. There is no such thing as time and distance to the subconscious.

Now this has all been scientifically proven, but to help participants in my workshops "get it" in the physical sense, on a personal level, I will often lead everyone on the guided journey I shared previously to imagine that they are sucking on a lemon. Ninety-five percent of the class will have a physical reaction to this visualization. Either their mouth will water, they'll taste or smell the lemon, or even have a physical shiver.

Maybe just thinking about this right now is having an affect on you.

I cannot emphasize enough the importance of your imagination combined with positive emotions to create and access infinite levels of experience and levels of your multi-dimensional self. But, it works both ways. Be very cautious about what you are imagining. If you imagine the worst, you are capable of creating that outcome and probably will. Typically, when we are imagining negative experience, we are giving in to our fears. There is no room for fear when you live as your Soul-self. The two energies cannot co-exist. When living life as your Soul, your dominate energy frequency is of love and trust.

The good news is that you can choose to create what you desire. Whatever you focus on, is what you will get more of. First get into your Soul-self state of energy. How do you do this? Your imagination, of course. Imagine that you are your Soul, that you will experience everything from the wisdom and love of your soul, and it will be true. Decide to consciously create what you desire and avoid imagining what you do not. The power to have all that you desire and to feel amazing all of the time, lives within you and your imagination is the doorway.

Key 6 – Everything is Energy

"All matter originates and exists only by virtue of a force…We must assume behind this force the existence of a conscious and intelligent Mind. This Mind is the matrix of all matter."

Max Planck, 1944 – Nobel Prize Winner – Physics 1918. Known as the father of Quantum Physics.

Everything in our world is vibrating energy. Photons or light, is the stuff our world is made of. It is a complete illusion that anything we see is solid. Denser things, like tables, cars, and rocks, for example, vibrate at a slower rate or lower level than more animated things like people, plants, animals and even crystals.

I heard it said once that if we were to condense the actual matter of the human body into its smallest measurement, releasing all that is space, the entire physical body would fit on the head of a pin. So basically, all we are is energy.

Because everything is made of energy, everything and everyone is connected and part of the whole. Since energy never dies, it only transforms, we are immortal energy beings.

A stream of light, pure love and intelligence flows within each of us. When this stream of light flows freely through us, we feel good, we feel joyful and fulfilled. We are eternal, timeless beings of light, connected with everyone and everything around us.

Unfortunately, most of us are asleep or "unconscious" of our true nature and spend our lives with barely a trickle of this pure potential and knowledge of who we really are and what we are truly capable of.

In the book The Divine Matrix by Gregg Braden, he discusses several scientific experiments that basically prove that we are energy and not only that, but our thoughts and our emotions have a direct effect on ourselves, on each other and on the world around us.

In addition, in Dr. Masaru Emoto's provocative work – Hidden Messages in Water, we can explore how our thoughts, words, pictures, even music affect water and therefore the world around us. When we consider that our bodies consist of mostly water as our world does, this has far reaching implications.

Dr. Emoto has had a lifelong fascination with water and began running experiments to determine how water lives and breathes. He began to say words to water, freeze it and then photograph the water. What he found is breathtaking. Water that was exposed to loving and kind words, classical music and photographs of dolphins, for example, formed beautiful, intricate crystals, like snowflakes.

Water that was exposed to negative, hateful words, created chaotic ice forms and ugly looking patterns. I highly recommend you explore Dr. Emoto's work. It is fascinating and beautiful and shows how we interact with our environment in a much more intimate way than we ever thought. It is more evidence that our thoughts, our words, music and beauty causes changes to our bodies. We can apply this knowledge to heal and create phenomenal health and well-being.

Energy Never Dies…It Only Transforms

In another experiment, scientists placed photons (light) in a vacuum sealed container. The photons appeared to die. After a period of time the photons came back to life, but had changed formation.

Another experiment shows the affect of DNA on the photons. Photons were again placed in a vacuum sealed container. The photons filled the container in a random pattern. Human DNA was placed in the container. The photons took on the exact shape of the DNA. The DNA was then removed. Scientists expected the photons to go back to their original pattern, but they didn't. The photons maintained the shape of the DNA after the DNA was removed. (To find out more about these experiments, I suggest reading the Divine Matrix, by Gregg Braden.)

What we can conclude: Our emotions affect our DNA and time and space is irrelevant. Our DNA affects light, or photons, which is what our entire world is made of, including our physical bodies. Our thoughts and imagination create our emotions and affect the water, our DNA, and light. Our bodies and our world are 75% water, 100% light or energy.

Additionally, think about this for a moment: when you breathe, cough or shake someone's hand, and basically just during the process of living and breathing, our DNA gets onto and into other people, animals, plants and things.

Our thoughts, and our feelings literally affect the world we live in, including ourselves and everything immediately around us and everywhere, all the time, regardless of distance.

New Age mumbo jumbo – I don't think so.

Do your thoughts create your reality? Yep!

Is it time to take back control of your consciousness and your emotional state? – double Yep!

It is only through our willingness to accept responsibility for how we think and feel, and heal the emotional wounds, subconscious beliefs, programs and ego trauma, that we will truly change the world around us. It starts within us. We cannot do this for anyone other than ourselves. We can only lead by example. The best gift you can give your loved ones and the world is creating a life that works, that is filled with joy and healthy relationship with ourselves and the Divine. Remember what I said earlier, we cannot give anyone what we do not have within us. Also, you will not find anything outside of yourself without looking within first.

It is critical that we heal ourselves, get out of blame and the victim mentality in order to heal the world and create peace on Earth.

Key 7 – Forgiveness! Set Your Spirit Free

Whenever we hold onto grievances, resentments or how someone did us wrong or treated us unfairly, we create a powerful energy hold in the subconscious part of our mind. This powerful energy hold blocks the flow of divine light through our energy systems, creating blocks in our physical, emotional and mental energy bodies.

These blocks then keep us from moving forward in the direction of our goals, keeping us stuck in negative thinking and negative energy. Energy is vibrating and vibration attracts more of the same or like vibration. This is called resonance. If our energy vibration is low and dense, our thoughts and emotions will be of a low, dense nature. We will attract more negative energy and experiences to us which can keep us from manifesting what we truly desire in our lives.

Unfortunately, when we feel betrayed the ego is activated in a struggle of loss and gain. We become "the victim." This keeps us from the higher vibrations of energy, where we are in the flow of love and light.

The subconscious mind does not know the difference between feelings you have about someone else and feelings you have toward yourself. If you are holding onto negative thoughts and feelings about another, you are holding these thoughts about yourself as well. There is no distinction in the subconscious. So poisonous thoughts are poisoning you too. We have already discussed what negative thoughts and emotions do to us physically, mentally and emotionally. So is it important to release our grudges and forgive? Critically so.

I have been a hypnotherapist and soul discovery coach for the last 15 years and I've seen over and over again how anger and resentment keep people stuck in their misery, and in their disease, sometimes manifesting physically. This kind of negative energy within will block the good that is available to you and from truly creating the life you desire and deserve.

Let's face it – grudges and resentments are a form of needing to be right and make someone else wrong. Feeling betrayed is a form of being offended. These three things we know for sure do not lead to happiness. When you forgive and let go, when you give yourself permission to be happy regardless of another's behavior towards you, you set yourself free.

Ego consciousness which resides in the less than 5% conscious level of your mind feeds on the need to be right. Ego consciousness will never be the path to happiness or what we desire. It completely blocks us from the flow of divine energy and unlimited universal love and wisdom that is available through the subconscious mind. The ego keeps us stuck in victim mentality perpetuating old programs that are self-defeating and will sabotage every effort to find real happiness.

How do you know if you are operating from ego consciousness and in a state of unforgiveness?

When you look at a situation and you find yourself having conversations in your mind, like a broken record, about what you should have said, or what you're going to say later to tell that person or show that person the way it is, your ego has taken over.

Whenever you get offended by someone's behavior or what they've said to you or others and you feel the need to defend yourself or your position. That is the ego.

Blame. Whenever you blame someone else or something else for your circumstances, your ego is pointing the finger, which is another aspect of the need to be right.

Ask yourself: Do you want to be right or do you want to be happy?

Sometimes I'll hear, "well it makes me happy to be right." (my teenagers.) But if you really think about that kind of momentary glee, you find it is fleeting and there's kind of a bad aftertaste a few moments or a few hours later because it is stuck in the ego level of consciousness. I know when I have done this from the sinking feeling I get in my gut or Solar Plexes Chakra. (We will discuss this in a later chapter.)

Then the guilt comes. You may not even know why you're feeling guilt, but it's inevitable whenever we pump ourselves up at the expense of someone else.

Guilt is an incredibly negative emotion, which decreases our energy vibration drastically into an unhealthy level. Remember, everything in our world is energy vibration. As we've already discussed in the chapter on energy, negative emotions and behaviors literally affect our bodies and our world.

By learning the power of forgiveness, by learning to forgive others, we begin to release these negative energy manifestations. Forgiveness is an incredible thing, it can also be very challenging. There is a correct way to utilize this amazing tool, a true releasing, and there's a way that seems great on the surface, but still has an element of ego consciousness within it. Be careful.

The true way takes some serious courage and it begins by being completely honest with ourselves. Are we really being accountable? Are we accepting even the slightest amount of responsibility for the situation at hand?

Based upon the Law of Attraction, every experience you've ever had is due to something magnetic within you, based upon your own thinking, your own experiences and beliefs, as we've discussed. It is called your Soul or Divine Self, there is an unseen part of you that has the desire to learn something so that you may grow and evolve. In the Spirit world, where the aspect of our Soul resides, outside of our physical bodies, we are all equal, here for the exact same purpose, to evolve and grow. Each person in physical form is here to experience their life lessons, in the process of remembering who they really are. When you can take a step back and observe each person from this perspective, there really isn't anything to forgive, because every experience is orchestrated from a higher level of consciousness for us to move forward on our life journey.

When challenging people and situations occur in my life, (and they do, but not as much now,) I now ask what belief I have that may have attracted the experience or the person. I come from a place of gratitude for the opportunity that has presented itself, in the form of this other person or situation, to clear out more limiting beliefs and subconscious programs that may be holding me back from even more joy.

If there is something you cannot forgive, you must start asking the question: How did I create this situation?

How can I begin to let it go? What am I to learn from this experience?

Keep in mind, that if you are feeling stuck or adamant about what someone did wrong to you, you are hooked into ego consciousness. There is often a part of us that is reluctant to "give up" on the grudge or betrayal. The ego likes to hold onto suffering and what it believes it should have. Remember, the ego loves to be right and holding a grudge is a form that this energy can take. It serves no part of you and will plug the flow of love and light energy where joy truly is and is accessed. The Soul-self knows nothing of betrayal.

Meditate on forgiveness and love in your heart while doing your breathing exercise. Forgiveness means letting the whole thing go, without any further attachment. Often this will come in layers. But begin the process. Keep digging deeper within yourself, because that is where the energy originates, not from the situation that you perceive as originating outside of you. Betrayal, forgiveness, this is your opportunity to grow to the next level.

Author Doreen Virtue has an excellent releasing statement that I also find very useful in shifting any unforgiveness:

"I release the part within me that gets irritated when I think of you."

Kind of funny, but very effective!

Here is a beautiful quote from Neale Donald Walsch, author of the Conversations with God series: "God Wants You to Know"

<u>*..that nothing is ever as bleak as it looks. Everything, in fact, is a blessing.*</u>

I know, I know...that is sometimes very hard to believe. How can a suddden, calamitous event in one's life be a blessing? It takes a longer view, I know, to see this wonderful truth. Even a diagnosis of a terminal illness could be seen as another gift from life wh en experienced from a particular perspective.

It is an opportunity for us to express once again, at the next highest level, Who We Really Are. And, if it turns out that, at the Soul level, we have indeed decided to leave our present physicality in this particular way and time, that, too, would be an expression of our Highest Self. And so, all "calamities" are blessings, not yet understood by the Mind. God knew this was a good day for you to hear this...

Love, Your Friend....

Even "calamitous" events and health challenges present an opportunity for us to grow from the perspective of the Soul. Every experience is a blessing designed for you to explore, to forgive and to find the gift.

By taking this first step, by accepting responsibility for every experience whether perceived as good or bad is a very important step in the path to forgiveness and to self healing.

Next, asking some great questions, without blame, how you may have contributed to the situation from your own past conditionings, beliefs and skewed perceptions. Someone cannot annoy or aggravate you without your permission. Consider that something inside of you and your belief system has become activated. You must give your permission to be offended by someone else. And the ego thrives on adversity.

Holding onto a grudge is negative energy that keeps paying dividends, over and over again. Feeling sorry for your circumstances works in the same negative way.

Remember, it is the ego that gets offended and the ego's primary function is to create drama. By creating drama, the ego tries to substantiate its own existence, its own importance, which again, will never allow you to experience true happiness. So this next step can be very insightful and help keep you from falling into the same trap again.

After doing your deep breathing exercise, (Key 2) and quieting your ego mind, use a powerful releasing statement such as: "I release all grudges, judgments, disappointments and resentments in all directions of time and space. I forgive and release everyone with whom I have ever perceived having harmed me in any way. We are now free and clear forever!"

Realize that everyone is entitled to their own opinion. Some people love to spew their opinions and ideas all over you. It is your choice how or whether you respond.

Make a decision right now to be happy no matter what is going on around you or even directed at you. Smile and just say that's interesting. Breathe. Become more aware of when you are offended and take a step back, observe, and make a different choice.

I'd love to hear your insights about forgiveness and how it has worked in your life.

Please email me directly or make a post on my blog about the Power of Forgiveness.

Key 8 – The Power of Gratitude

Gratitude–noun

the quality or feeling of being grateful or thankful.

"I know how to summarize your chapter on gratitude in one word – ***Thanks!***" James Deegan

My friend James is correct if not concise (and maybe just a little bit silly!) Giving thanks is the beginning of attracting higher level things, people and experiences to you.

So how does it work?

As we discussed in Key 1 – Harness the Power of Your Own Mind, your subconscious mind instantly registers your thoughts, in fact every thought you have, consciously or unconsciously. So this is of course, also true regarding your thoughts and feelings about gratitude. The subconscious will search through all of your experiences, memories, and programs to give you matching or like feedback to support you with whatever you're thinking about, which in this case – things you're thankful or grateful for.

All of your experiences, past feelings, beliefs and blocks that are created are stored in the subconscious part of your mind – right down to the cellular level. Your consciousness is literally in every cell in your body. Also, it does not know the difference between what is real or what you imagine. It makes no judgment, it only registers the thoughts and feelings, finds a match from your past experiences and beliefs, then gives you more of that thought or feeling. Very much like a computer – garbage in, garbage out! Good stuff in, good stuff out!

Are you beginning to realize how much power you really have over your circumstances, well at least how you feel at any time, regardless of your circumstances? I hope so and that is my goal for you and why I wrote this book.

Whatever you think about you get more of. Add emotion to what you're thinking and wham, you have the combination to create anything you desire and to feel happy all the time if you so choose.

We've discussed in some detail that our world and everything in it, including us, is vibrating energy – vibrating atoms, subatomic particles and photons or light, to be precise. Energy vibration is like a magnet for more energy which has the same vibrational frequency or resonance. So of course, our thoughts and feelings are also energy with their own frequency and are very magnetic. The more positive and loving the thought or emotion, the higher the vibration. The more negative, fearful or depressing a thought or emotion…well you get the idea. Whatever the frequency, it will attract more of the same or like frequencies.

So what does this mean?

As we express gratitude for what we have already attracted, we become a vibrational match to more of that, which we are grateful for. We are in essence giant magnets, attracting to us more of the energy vibration that correlates to *our* energy or vibrational frequency. Our thoughts, feelings and vibration attract to us the synchronistic events, people, opportunities and things which are in harmony *with* our vibration.

The key to this is feeling. Emotions are the true barometer of what we are attracting. So it is important to feel sincere about what you are grateful for. It is crucial to think positive thoughts that create happy emotions. The happier you feel, the higher level people, things and situations you will attract.

I know I sound redundant, however, this is so important I want to make sure you receive the concept from every angle until it becomes a part of you.

When we focus on gratitude, we literally change the way we view things, our thoughts about circumstances and people and ultimately how we can allow ourselves to receive more good feelings and more good things. When we receive more good things and good feelings we feel happy!

Our number one priority in life, *is* to be happy. If that's not true for you, then it should be, based on what I've shared with you. It is your responsibility to stay in a joyful state because your energy literally affects the world. I assume, if you weren't looking for a way to be happy more of the time, you probably wouldn't be reading this book.

"When you change the way you look at things, the things you look at, change." **Dr. Wayne Dyer**

I was recently listening to an audio CD that was created by the editorial director and publisher of Success Magazine, Darren Hardy.

He describes in detail how gratitude can change your life in the area of your relationships. A friend of his was complaining about his own wife and how she wasn't this and wasn't that. Basically, he was making her responsible for his own state of happiness. Conversely, Darren's perception was that she was a terrific lady and his friend was lucky to have her.

That Thanksgiving, Darren Hardy decided to keep a gratitude journal about his own wife for an entire year. Each day, for a few moments, he wrote down something about her that he was grateful for, whether it was how she looked beautiful that day, how she interacted with the kids, or cooked a great meal.

His intention to be grateful allowed him to begin to notice the subtleties, characteristics and qualities that he might not have been aware of before if he had remained focused on her surface attributes. As he focused on his wife's positive aspects, he found himself falling deeply in love with her all over again. And because of the wonderful feelings toward her that his gratitude created, she began to respond to him in a more loving way, which contributed greatly to their overall relationship, elevating it to an entirely new and different level.

Darren suggested that his friend try this technique and within just a few months, his friend felt completely different about his own wife. Instead of complaining about her, he found himself appreciating all that she contributed to their relationship and their lives. Of course, she responded positively to *his* change and they saved their marriage.

This is the power of gratitude in just this one area. The same is true of everything in your life. Imagine for a moment how sincere heartfelt gratitude, for your health, your prosperity, your circumstances, your children, your job, etc. could change the energy within *you* and allow you to begin to experience everything from a higher wiser perspective. How will the people in your life respond? How will the universe respond?

There are two ways to begin to show gratitude that I will suggest here.

1. Upon waking every day or right before you fall asleep at night, make a mental list about all the things you are grateful for. Say it in your own mind or say it out loud. Begin with: "I am grateful for ___________."
2. Keep a gratitude journal each and every day and actually write down everything you are grateful for. It can be as simple as, "I am grateful for the air in my lungs."

You don't have to take a long time to do this. Just write down 2 or 3 things each day. What you'll find is the more you do this, the more things you'll find to be grateful for. It's amazing. You will attract more wonderful things to you as you show more and more gratitude and the people in your life will be uplifted by your rasied energy vibration. What a huge gift in a such simple thing.

A joyful life is really very simple: stay out of drama, don't get offended, think only joyful thoughts, forgive yourself and others for so-called trespasses or "mistakes" and be grateful for all the wonders around and within you.

Key 9 – Joy – A Way of Life

Based on what we've discussed so far, I hope by now you realize that you will be happy when you decide to and will accept nothing less.

Happiness is your divine right. It's so easy to get caught up in the things in our world that bring us down. Massive amounts of people thrive on negativity to give them something to focus on, other than their own lives and sometimes even to pump themselves up. This is why the news and media focus on everything that's going wrong, who's wrong and what we should think about them.

Advertising is focused on why you're not good enough and how buying their product will make you all better.

Again, that is ego consciousness and is the antithesis of the path of Joy and Living a Soul life!

So by now you already have many tools to utilize and new understandings about the nature of our world of energy and the power inherent in your own subconscious mind, so you can make different choices about how you think and feel personally. To change our world, we must start with ourselves. It is my hope and goal that you can appreciate the value of taking good care of yourself and deciding to be happy. When you give yourself permission to stay in a higher flow of joy, your good feelings and high vibration literally raise the energy around you.

Since we now know, our thinking, emotions and inner happiness spreads to everything and everyone else, our number one priority is to create inner harmony, to connect with the God within and find our joy, our passion, our spirit. As we radiate self love, self esteem and joy, which comes from within and from our Soul or Higher Self, we truly affect the world around us in a positive way.

There is no way to fake this either. No amount of fake smiles and pretend joy are going to work. Energy knows the truth and subconsciously, since we are all connected, so does everyone else, on some level. However, I am a believer in "fake it 'til you make it" because your subconscious doesn't know the difference and will set into motion all the forces necessary for manifestation, and from one moment to the next, you may be pleasantly surprised to find yourself actually feeling joyful. So smile anyway. Your subconscious mind doesn't know the difference and you'll notice that it's very difficult to stay sad or angry when you're smiling.

There really are no excuses. Evolve or die. It's that simple.

We are experiencing a major shift in human consciousness. More and more people on our planet are realizing that the status quo just isn't working anymore. More and more people are realizing their intuitive gifts than ever before, (which is one of the gifts of the subconscious.) The realization that we are all connected on this one planet is coming more into the conscious awareness than ever before. There is no "us" and "them" anymore and those who continue along *that* path, will soon find destruction and devastation.

Although, there is more disaster and global negativity, probably more than ever before in our history, there is also a movement, if you will, of those souls who say: "enough!" to our two-faced politicians, "enough!"

polluting our environment and "enough" greed and selfish agendas of bloated corporations.

"Enough!" of school systems that don't work, that do not encourage a child's inherent gifts, that force children to regurgitate outdated ideas. "Enough" of underpaid, overwhelmed teachers. We need a new paradigm in the school system that celebrates a child's unique contribution, builds self-esteem and teaches true wealth and how to function successfully, intelligently and responsibly in a capitalistic, democratic and morally sound society. Children should not be pigeoned holed into one way of thinking, regurgitating information that may be completely irrelevant to their innate gifts, talents and their "Soul" purpose.

Many people are asking what has happened to ethics and values? There's an attitude of entitlements, blame and pointing fingers.

It's time for us to accept responsibility for our own lives and our own experiences.

Learning to take responsibility for your own thinking and feeling and making a decision to be happy is a great example for our children. Living as your Soul, connected with Source is the key. Health and wellness begins at home and radiates out into our society. Living a Soul Life means you no longer expect things outside yourself to provide your education or your security.

And since we now know that everything is energy, everything is connected, our primary purpose is to maintain our inner health and to put our focus on the beauty and love that is within us and all around us.

Although it's very easy to get sucked into the negativity, into the discussions about what is wrong in the world, the best thing you can do is focus on what is love, what is beauty, making that Soul connection every day and feeling good from the inside out. This is how you will really make a difference and the big bonus for you is...you get to be happy!

A dear friend of mine (who shall remain anonymous) and a very enlightened person once told me that she doesn't watch any television and she doesn't say any negative words whatsoever. I asked her how that was possible. I was curious how she would know if something bad happened or not.

Her answer stuck with me ever since. She replied, if something bad happened, there's really nothing she could do about it anyway. So if it is the end of the world, for example, "I'll be happy to the very last moment."

With her intention to stay joyful no matter what, to speak the language of the subconscious and live her life from the Soul level, my friend has created a wonderful, successful life for herself. She utilizes many of the practices I have shared here to help her navigate through some difficult and challenging times. Without placing blame, but by accepting responsibility for every experience as an opportunity to grow and evolve, she passed through those challenges very quickly and has now attracted a wonderful relationship, a beautiful home, a successful, prosperous business and plenty of positive and loving friends.

This is the perfect example of Living a Soul Life and you can do it too.

You Are the Designer of Your Destiny

You came into this world with a vibration or energy frequency that is the dominant energy of who you are in this lifetime, and what your Soul has determined you will accomplish in your personal growth.

From the Soul's Perspective, there is truly no such thing as failure, only growth and learning.

This is so that you may evolve to the next stage. What that next stage is, we probably will never understand from the limited physical perspective. It is really beyond most of our human understanding.

As an intelligent collection of conscious particles in this Universe, you are what the Creator-God/Goddess, the All That Is, is doing in human form. Your thoughts and feelings literally create and affect the world around us and everything in it. We are connected to everything and everyone through a matrix of energy, an intelligent field, "a conscious and intelligent Mind" (as Max Planck described years ago) as the essence of the energy connection or "Universal Mind" of "All That Is." As a collection of conscious energy particles we are actually Co-Creators of this reality in each and every moment. Everything around us exists, including us, as part of this "Universal Mind." This un-manifest essence is the substance out of which all physical form, or the illusion of solid form, is created.

The Universal Mind is perfection. It perfectly creates what you think about!

Orin

Your subconscious mind is a gateway to the Universal Mind where we are all connected and where you have access to all information anywhere and all the time. Your intuition is one of the aspects of the subconscious. Everyone has access to it. It is not unique to the "gifted."

Focus on what you desire to create, not what you don't want. Whatever you focus on or think about, your subconscious will respond! Remember, the subcsoncsious mind will not judge what you think about, it will just respond with feedback, bringing to you more of what you think about. Since your subconscious is the gateway to the Universal Mind, when you are in a relaxed or meditative state, you have direct access to the All That Is, the Collective Unconscious, where anything you desire to create or know resides as pure energy with pure potential to become whatever you wish.

Your creativity and imagination are the two most important elements in creating what you desire. Combine them with a quiet and peaceful mind and a high physical energy vibration and you have the perfect blend for manifestation.

How do you create a high physical vibration?

There are 4 different ways to increase your energy vibration:

- Eating a healthy diet of fresh fruits, vegetables, and foods that have energy and light, avoiding dense foods, animal proteins, acidic foods, sugar, etc. Create a ph balanced body! (There are plenty of books about this and you can find more information on my blog. http://www.suziebowers.com.)
- Exercise daily – get out in nature too. Exercise itself releases endorphins and other powerful brain chemicals that automatically make you feel good. Moving your body, helps to relieve stress, which assists your mind to naturally be more positive. Taking nature walks in all kinds of weather is energizing – focus on all the

beauty and miracles in the world around you. Appreciate what is naturally loving, abundant and beautiful about our world.

- Meditate everyday! 20 or 30 minute guided visualization or breathing and quieting the mind is the key to connecting with the All That Is and in raising your vibration. Practice daily being grateful for what you have and the beauty all around you.
- Begin to get to know and play with Light! Because you are energy and our world is vibrating energy or light, just by thinking of light it will respond to you. Imagine you are calling light to yourself, breathe it in, imagine it is filling you up. Feels Great! (We'll be exploring this in detail in the next chapter.

Become very clear about what brings you joy and then settle for nothing less. You came here to be a unique contributor to this world. Follow your passion, do what you love and you'll find doors opening for you that you weren't even aware of before.

Key 10 –Becoming Conscious – Connecting to Your Soul

Light is one of the most powerful forces in the universe, if not *"the"* most powerful force. Love is the force that moves and animates light. As we've previously discussed, light is what our universe is made of, it is everywhere and anywhere all the time. It is everything and within everyone. It is a living presence. You are light. Light has a high energy vibration or frequency. Different colors radiate or resonate at different frequencies. For example, white light is one of the highest frequencies, with a finer vibration than other colors. Play with the colors and find out what feels good to you.

As you think of light you begin to vibrate as your Soul-self or "Higher Self." With your intention and imagination, visualize and feel that you are connecting and becoming your Soul-self as if it were real, because it is.

As you make this connection at a conscious level, with your intention, you begin to awaken to the reality of the energy world, meaning you are becoming conscious.

By becoming conscious, you are no longer shrouded by the illusion of false reality – or the world of fear. You begin to understand that we live in an energy world, that appearances are not real. Begin to focus on the feeling sense of things and how things flow through you energetically. As you accept responsibility for every experience and look for an opportunity to grow, instead of blame, you will begin to experience life from the loving lens of the the Soul-self.

Moving through life as your Higher Self or Soul-self allows you to feel good more of the time, to attract better things into your life, and to create your experience in the highest and best way for you, which in turn creates beautiful energy shared with the rest of the world.

There is a Flow of Life Force Throughout and Beyond the Body

Scientists at the Institute of Heartmath have discovered a magnetic field they within and around the heart. The hypothesis is that it is the heart that is the processing center of our bodies, not the brain as previously believed. The electromagnetic field they have discovered is the heart chakra and is part of a system or network of energy which is who we really are, within us and extending to and a part of infinity or All That Is.

The "aura" is the electro-magnetic field that is truly us. It is the combination of all the energy centers or chakras. We have and live within many bodies other than just our physical manifestation. We are a complete, all-emcompassing body of energy and consciousness. It is this energy which is immortal and temporarily housed within a physical being. We consist of a mental body, an emotional body and the essence of our Soul-selves, the Light Body.

The physical body is the organic computer that our spirit uses to walk in the physical world. One day our organic shelter will die and return to dust, or "nothing" but our energy will live on, eternally.

Each energy center or chakra* has its own frequency, color and is connected to the others. For example:

(The heart center radiates a green light, which has a frequency.)

*"Chakra means Wheel of Light. It is an ancient Sanskrit term."

As each energy center or chakra radiates frequency and emits color, they are spinning and balancing, constantly fluctuating with our emotional and mental health. Each is connected, to the organs and nervous system of our body, the "consciousness" if you will. There are many chakras within and beyond the physical body. There are 7 main chakras that are essential in maintaining balance and well-being. These spinning energy vortices are connected with our emotional and mental energy bodies, which are typically not seen by the human eye. This system, the aura, is very much like a CPU, the Central Processing Unit of our bodies.

The aura is the "rainbow bridge" that connects us to the spiritual dimension, our higher selves/soul selves and who we really are. In addition, these energy centers also interact with nature and other beings, whether physical or non-physical. The body is an illusion, it is literally an organic computer that houses our spirit. Our energy fields are part of the entire whole of the universe or actually the "multi-verse."

What's important to know, is that our thoughts and emotions affect our energy field, in fact certain emotions have a direct affect on different chakras that in turn affect our body.

The first chakra which is located in between the anus and genitals is called the Root Chakra and is associated with the consciousness surrounding security, survival, prosperity issues. The color of the Root Chakra is a deep ruby red. The Root Chakra opens downward like a funnel into the earth and is our grounding center and connection to our Mother, the earth.

The second chakra is the Sacral Chakra and it is associated with the energies of sexuality, procreation, creativity and nurturing emotions. It is located between the navel and genitals and the color is Orange.

The third chakra is the Solar Plexes Chakra and it is related to Power and Control. It is literally located in the upper part of the abdomen and the color is a bright sunny yellow.

The fourth chakra is the Heart Chakra and is located near the heart, but in the center of the chest. The Heart

Chakra radiates an emerald green energy and is associated with love and acceptance and issues of the heart.

The fifth chakra is called the Throat Chakra. The color of robins egg blue, the Throat Chakra relates to voice, creativity, speaking our truth and knowledge. It is located at the throat.

The sixth chakra is the Third Eye Chakra, located between and above the eyes, in the middle of the forehead. The color is Royal Blue and the energy is associated with clear vision or seeing the truth. This energy center is also concerned with Clairvoyance, or seeing beyond the physical senses, multi-dimensionally.

The seventh chakra is the Crown Chakra and is the color of royal purple. It is located at the top of the head like a crown. This vortex of energy opens upward like a funnel into the world of spirit. It is the connection, gateway or union with our Soul or Divine Selves and the All That Is.

It is these spinning vortices of energy that comprise the dynamic of our energy field or aura. It is this energy field that reacts to the energies of the world, other people, our own thoughts and emotions, the spiritual dimension and ultimately has an affect on our physical body. Learning to meditate with these energies is a fantastic way to stay in balance and maintain a stronger connection with our Divine or Soul-self.

Activating the Light Body

As beings of Light, it is possible to activate the Light Body through a series of higher energy centers, centers that exist in a higher dimension than the chakras. The chakras are the bridge, as I mentioned. The light body is what "they" talk about when Jesus Christ ascended. "The Ascension" is when we all do it. There have been other Master Beings that have ascended from the earth plane. Jesus is the most well known.

Since Everything is Energy and We are Made of Light, You can Instantly Access the Soul by Bringing in Light.

Use this new knowledge, this ability to play with light to create what you desire. As you think of light, it automatically draws to you because you *are* light. It increases your vibration and that vibration radiates to everyone and everything around you, making you very attractive to more good.

Send light out to other people, to things you desire and to your own body and the world around you.

- **As you breathe deeply, imagine right now that you are standing in a sparkling shower of light that is flowing down from God or as high up in the universe as you can imagine, and that your body and energy field are absorbing this beautiful energy. Imagine the light is washing away any negativity or discomfort from your body. Connecting with light can rejuvenate your body at the cellular level and increase the energy that is available to you.**
- **Take another deep breath and with your intention, imagine that the divine you, your Soul/Higher Self are becoming one with you.**
- **Light is filling every part of your being now. You may feel a vibration or a tingle, the**

feeling of warmth spreading through you or even a chill in your body. You may even receive pictures in your mind or hear a high pitched or beautiful sound. You may experience colors of light in your mind's eye.

You may feel nothing and that's ok too. Your thought and intention is all that is required and it is done.

- **Now imagine that you are surrounded by a bubble or a sphere of light that is all around you, like a cocoon of light. Do this every day before you move out into the world. This will automatically increase your energy vibration which will in turn attract more good to you and protect you from undesirable thoughts and energy.**
- **Bring your awareness to your heart center. Put your hand on your chest and say to your heart: "I love you." Breathe deeply as the light flows into your heart center and radiates pure love into your body and out into the world. Observe how you feel. Pay attention to any slight or powerful shift within you.**

You are the co-creator of your reality. You can accomplish anything you can imagine. Know within every cell of your being, that if you can imagine something then it is possible for you to create it. Don't let anyone tell you that you cannot do something. God's manifestation through you is unique to you. No one else can possibly know why you are here. That is very personal and between you and the divine you. Just like snowflakes, each one of manifested on the earth plane are unique. Your DNA is unique to you, yet we are all One from the same Source of All That Is. Respect each and every being as here to have their own experience which is being divinely guided at all times by the Soul-self. What your Soul has determined you are here to learn, may be different from anothers journey. Don't feel sorry for anyone's experiences. Bless each person and realize they are also the creators of their own reality.

When others give you their opinions they are operating from "ego consciousness." This keeps them from being responsible for their own path and passion, which does not serve anyone. Don't judge.

Recognize this, send them love and be on your way. They can't help it because they are not becoming conscious, like you, at least not yet. When you honor your passions and purpose in life, you give subconscious permission, inspiration really, for other souls to do the same. What a true gift!

Choose to be happy always. Choose to live your life with passion and follow the whisperings of joy that live within your heart. You are here for a purpose. As Dr. Wayne Dyer says, "don't die with your song still inside you."

I look forward to hearing about your success. Please let me know how you're doing, how you liked this book and remember – You Can Create the Life You Desire and Deserve, which is Unlimited!

Conclusion

The ancient mystics and native peoples have known in their hearts and their spirits for thousands of years, about the interconnection of all life and that this planet and everything in it and around it is a living, breathing organism, that we are all One.

Science has now proven what was known all along.

In our astonishing growth over the last 2000 and specifically the past 150 years, we have forgotten. Ancient spiritual teachings have been lost or twisted around to serve the egos of men. In our race for technology and world domination, we are losing our world to greed, the need to be right, depletion of our resources, power and corruption. Food is contaminated due to over use of pesticides and hormones. In the name of greed and production, we have altered the very nature of our food genetically and destroyed our earth's ability to grow what we need sustain us in a natural and loving environment.

We must stop looking outside ourselves for answers. We must start to accept responsibility for how the chaos in our inner world, inside our very beings, and our disconnection with all that is natural and loving, has manifested into the outer world.

If our emotions affect our DNA and our DNA affects the stuff our world is made of, the only conclusion we can draw is that becoming conscious of how we think and feel is paramount to the survival of our world. We ourselves, within ourselves must be the change that we seek outside of us.

Sit still and tune into the inner most whisperings and stirrings inside you. There is an inner wisdom, within your soul, your subconscious and within your own body that is ever present, guiding you and urging you to live your life with joy and passion. This you that is connected with All That Is, is never ending, all loving and available to you at all times.

Your soul has all the answers you will ever need to be the physical you at your highest and best level. Let go of the garbage, let go of the victim. You are not a victim. You are a spiritual being having a human experience.

You are far greater than you even know.

We all have subconscious programs that can be self-defeating and can keep us stuck in repeating patterns. By tapping into this inner wisdom, we can release and change those patterns into supportive processes.

Breathe deeply and decide to let that stuff go. It does not serve you. Release it and focus on what you desire to bring into your life, what you desire to create for yourself. You are the co-creator of everything. And there are no limits to what you can do. Limits are self-imposed and in our own mind.

Make a mental connection with your soul right now and listen to the gentle nudges and inner stirrings that your soul is utilizing to guide you on your way.

By starting each day connecting with your soul, you can truly live a soul life and create the life you desire and deserve.

How do I personally feel joyful and happy most of the time. First, I have decided that I want to and make a point of not settling for anything less. Meditation and exercise are my first priority almost every day. When things come up, because they do, I do my best to stay centered within my own being and connected with my Source.

By staying out of ego consciousness, (which is all about being offended and getting feelings hurt and judging others,) intend to maintain a strong connection with the divine being of love and light that you truly are. The planet is immersed in ego consciousness and the ego must create drama and fear in order to continue to substantiate its' own existence. Everything of the ego is an illusion. When you can really take a step back and observe the drama from your higher, divine self, you realize it is a bunch of So What?! Everything passes. And all that truly matters is the healing of ourselves and walking through this world maintaining our peaceful connection to the Divine All That Is, Mother/Father God, letting those things that are of the ego of others, flow around us. The shamans call this "being transparent," which means transparent to the negative, poisonous energies of others. It serves no one to engage the ego personality of others. The truth is 90% of humans do not even know what they are doing. They are infants on the earth plane, compared to who they really are. Just because you are reading this book, you are different. Something incredible is taking place within you for you to be attracted to this work.

All that matters is love and it must be "unconditional," which means no judgment, ever. That is what the great masters Jesus and Buddha and others, were talking about. Each soul is on their individual journey, and in that way we are all equal and that must be respected. Each soul will choose the path and the life circumstances, beliefs and perceptions, in which they will learn their lessons to evolve. And in these times, either evolve or die! A great shift is currently taking place on this planet as foretold by many ancient peoples. It is becoming more and more difficult to stay stuck in unconsciousness.

Today, as a rule, I avoid getting sucked into the ego personality, because that is the lie, and that includes getting tricked into any discussion of any kind that includes judgment or negativity. When I was younger, I could easily get into an argument and state my point of view. I would always take the other side of the topic, even if I wasn't sure I really believed in it. I learned later that getting involved in an argument, having to sway others to my point of view was a way to get energy. Unfortunately this energy was not from the Universal Source of Love and Light, but the energy of others.

Have you ever been around someone who loves to spew their opinion all over you or try to get you to make an opinion about something just to get you into an argument? Have you ever realized how drained you feel after being around that person?

The more you stay connected with your Divine Self or Soul Self and the Universal Source of All Love and Light, the more you realize you don't need to have an opinion about anything. You will have all you require energetically from the Source and it feels so much better. It feels real and true and it lasts. You will also be more sensitive to other people's energy and may find yourself avoiding others who drain you.

If you find yourself in the presence of someone's energy that does feel good to you use this quick and easy tool: In your mind, call the white light (heavenly-love-light) to yourself and surround yourself with a bubble of light, breathe and stay in your peaceful center. Because you are energy, all you have to do is think it and it is done. You may notice that the other person leaves in a few moments when, unconsciously, they realize they are not getting any energy from you.

My teachers have imparted to me to completely ignore the ego personality when it rears its ugly head within others, because to get engaged with that part of another human, only mutually feeds it (the ego.) That is the anti-thesis of enlightenment and the opposite of joy. To step back and observe that part of others (and ourselves, of course), is the opportunity presenting itself to face whatever belief is coming to the surface to be healed and transformed. I actually feel a kind of joy inside when I observe others' "stuff" coming to the surface, because I know that it is their opportunity to heal and release it. And it will take many of us to wake up and heal our programs to shift this planet to the next level. It is each person's choice, as we all have free will, to utilize the opportunities presented to grow or stay stuck. I have come to realize that judgment and emotional drama of others has nothing to do with me even when it seems to be directed *at* me.

Truth is, that nothing is personal and if I can stay out of taking anything personally, I can stay more connected with Source and out of ego drama.

My personal goal is to be happy all of the time. Therefore, I will not allow other's opinions to pull me off course for very long, if at all anymore. It's so amazingly refreshing. I just nod and say "Is that so?"

There is an old story of a village wiseman. He was accused of getting the neighbors daughter pregnant. When he was accused of this atrocity by the entire village, he did not defend himself, he just replied, “Is that so?”

After the child was born, the village folks delivered the child to the wiseman and told him since he did this foul thing, he must raise this child as his own. He replied, “Is that so?” He took the child and and began to raise him as his own.

Years later the girl who delivered the baby felt so guilty that she finally admitted it was not the wiseman but the baker’s son who she had indiscretions with and who was the father of the child.

They village people came to the wiseman and apologized for accusing him. He replied, “Is that so?”

The wiseman never allowed himself to get caught up in the ego drama, went about his business without any attachment.

The moral of the story is that everything passes, so why get caught up in the drama. None of this will matter later.

As many ways as there are to be in the world, as many grains of sand that exist in the world, there are as many opinions of others and as many pathways to God. So why bother, why spend a single moment trying to justify or defend yourself or tell another person that their point of view is wrong. It accomplishes nothing, but feeding the ego.

The important thing is to nourish and nurture your personal relationship with God, the Divine Source that lives within you. Together we can create Heaven on Earth and as we elevate our frequency away from negativity and separateness to a higher, finer vibration, we raise the collective consciousness of the entire planet.

This is a process and anyone can do it. It is your choice and divine right to be happy, to stay connected with your Source and to be a light for all the world to see.

Namaste'

In Love and Light,

Suzie

Helpful Affirmations

I am one with the divine presence of all life.

I radiate love and light to my body and the world around me.

I forgive myself and I love the being of light that I am.

I tune into my intuition where I am guided to be the best me.

I relax and let love and light flow through me with ease.

I am safe and protected by the light of God.

I feel love and I give love to everyone I come in contact with.

Abundance and vibrant health are my divine birthright.

I deserve and accept the very best that life offers.

Divine love and light flow through me and radiate out to the world.

Affirmations for Success

I am a contribution, my services are valuable.

I am able to ask for what I want.

I now attract prosperous and competent people who want to do business with me.

Every day I wake up to new wealth.

Money comes to me easily.

I am a money magnet.

All the money that I deserve by divine right comes to me now under grace and in a perfect way

Financial Success comes to me now.

Money flows to me easily and effortlessly.

I am highly capable.

I attract money from everywhere.

I am highly successful.

I am creating a loving life.

This is an abundant universe and there is plenty for all of us.

I deserve to be prosperous and happy. I am now prosperous and happy!

Financial success is coming to me easily and effortlessly.

I now have a satisfying income of $__________ per month, or more.

I am rich, well, and happy.

I am talented,

I am good enough.

I accept prosperity. and abundance into my life.

I expect only the best to happen and it does.

I am always in the right place at the right time for my success.

I trust and follow my inner guidance.

I am completely unlimited.

intelligent and creative I deserve the very best in life.

I easily make $__________

My value and worth are increased by everything I do.

Affirmations for Joy

Harmony, Peace, Love and Joy surround me and indwell in me. I am safe and secure. I am loved.

I am alive and filled with Joy.

I see life as eternal. I
am eternal and joyous
and at peace.

I relax and recognize
my self-worth.

I am good enough.
Life is easy and
Joyful.

I am free to circulate
love and joy in every
part of my world. I
love life.

I am one with all life. I
am safe at all times.

I release the past. I
forgive and forget. I
forgive myself.

I love and approve of

myself. I see myself
and what I do with
eyes of love.

I am healthy and
happy.

My body pulsates with
joy, happiness and
aliveness.

I bring joy and light
energy to the center of
my heart. I express
love.

I activate my inner
healer.

The heavenly, love,
light heals my heart
and circulatory
system.

I am safe. I trust in the process of life. Life is for me.

I am filled with strength, power and love.

I move forward in life with joy, love and ease.

I nourish and heal myself with the heavenly love light.

I am connected with universal love.

Resources

Gregg Braden, *The Divine Matrix: Bridging Time, Space, Miracles and Belief* (Carlsbad, CA: Hay House, 2007.)

Gregg Braden, *Speaking the Lost Language of God: Awakening the Forgotten Wisdom of Prayer, Prophecy and the Dead Sea Scrolls* audio series. (Niles, Illinois: Nightingale Conant.)

Dr. Wayne Dyer, *The Power of Intention: Learning to Co-create Your World Your Way* (Carlsbad, CA: Hay House, 2004.)

Sanaya Roman, *Spiritual Growth: Being Your Higher Self* (Tiburon, CA: HJ Kramer, 1989.)
http://www.orindaben.com

Masaru Emoto, *The Hidden Messages In Water,* (Hillsboro, Oregon: Beyond Words Publishing, Inc., 2004.)

Colin C. Tipping, *Radical Forgiveness, Making Room for the Miracle*, (Marietta, Georgia: Global 13 Publications Col, Trust, 1997.)

Dr. Joseph Murphy, Ph.D, *The Power of Your Subconscious Mind*, (Englewood Cliffs, N.J., 1963.)

Rhonda Byrne, *The Secret,* (Hillsboro, Oregon, 2006.)

About the Author

Suzie Bowers is a Certified Clinical Hypnotherapist and Soul Discovery Coach, Herbalist, Publisher, Marketing Consultant, Mother of 3, Grandmother and Friend.

She started her career in real estate and discovered the path to self improvement after a bad horse-back riding fall injured her head and neck and sent her into a deep depression. Medicine and traditional therapies didn't help. It was through hypnotherapy, the use of the relaxed state of mind called hypnosis together with Wisdom Center TechnologiesTM that Suzie had an "awakening" that changed her life.

During the hypnosis session Suzie found herself face to face with the most powerful light she'd ever experienced. From that point forward, the depression lifted and a whole new world, "the power of the mind and spirit" opened up to Suzie.

In 1995, Suzie spent 6 intensive months, 250 hours of hands on training at California Institute of the Healing Arts and Sciences, then more training at American Pacific University and Smoke Free International.

Being called to her roots, Suzie also began a shamanic practice, studying levels of consciousness that are beyond the 5 senses with author and shamanic trainer, Lynn V. Andrews. Observing the ways of "Spirit" in nature and exploring ancient spiritual teachings has added age-old wisdom to Suzie's skills and tools.

This also lead Suzie to exploring energy and the lightbody, an energy system that exists at a higher, finer dimension than the chakras and is a pathway to connection to Divine Source.

She has worked with people all over the world, to help them heal, connect with their own inner wisdom, live their passion and create the life they desire and deserve. Suzie also holds classes on meditation and divine light, soul connection, Angelic Reiki, and has a monthly spiritual drumming circle

Suzie is available to speak at your next event and does talks about Living a Soul Life and The Power of Your Mind to Create the Life You Desire and Deserve.

Upcoming Books by Suzie Bowers

Dragonfly: Journey Into Light

Create the Life You Desire and Deserve

Please visit Suzie's blog

http://www.suziebowers.com and sign up for her free Monday Morning Power Start series and newsletter.

If you'd like to contact Suzie for your next speaking event or a private session:

suziebowers@yahoo.com

800-758-1239

Notes:

33084723R00094

Made in the USA
San Bernardino, CA
24 April 2016